Family in Islamic Psychology Perspective:
Challenges and Solutions

Islamic Psychology and Biopsychological Basics of Life in Education and Health

Edited by
Dian Sari Utami, Emi Zulaifah and Marcus Stueck

Volume 2

PETER LANG

Muhammad Ali Ramdhani / Agus Abdul Rahman /
Nani Nuranisah Djamal / Asti Meiza (eds.)

Family in Islamic Psychology Perspective: Challenges and Solutions

PETER LANG

Lausanne - Berlin - Bruxelles - Chennai - New York - Oxford

Bibliographic Information published by the Deutsche Nationalbibliothek
The Deutsche Nationalbibliothek lists this publication in the Deutsche Nationalbibliografie; detailed bibliographic data is available online at http://dnb.d-nb.de.

Library of Congress Cataloging-in-Publication Data
A CIP catalog record for this book has been applied for at the Library of Congress.

Cover Illustration: © Canva

ISSN 2750-3968
ISBN 978-3-631-89457-6 (Print)
E-ISBN 978-3-631-89492-7 (E-PDF)
E-ISBN 978-3-631-89493-4 (E-PUB)
DOI 10.3726/b20477

Publicado por Peter Lang GmbH, Berlín, Alemania

info@peterlang.com - www.peterlang.com

This publication has been peer reviewed.

This book is dedicated to all families in the universe

Preface

This book was preceded by an International Conference on Family and Islamic Values held in Indonesia at 2019. Some of the presenters followed up the conference by writing articles and the conference committee combined it into this book chapter. This book summarizes the recent works on the study of psychology and family, particularly on how to strengthen the family and overcoming challenges that come in the way.

Foreword of the authors of the book

Alhamdulillah, all praise be to Allah Ta'ala because with His permission and power, this book chapters have been successfully completed and published. This book contains a collection of articles presented at the International Conference On Family and Islamic Value (ICON-FIVE) with the theme 'Family in Islamic Psychology Perspective: Challenges and Solutions' which was held on March 15-16 2019 at the Grand Aquilla Hotel Bandung, West Java, Indonesia. This book was published by Peter Lang Publisher as part of the book series 'Islamic Psychology and Biopsychological Basics of Life in Education and Health'.

The ICON-FIVE conference brought up several topics for call papers, namely family and environment; family and technology; family and economy; family and religion; family and society; family and law; family and culture; and family and education. The publication of this book is intended to disseminate the results of research related to families conducted by academics and researchers, particularly from the field of psychology.

Even though it took a long time to complete the process of publishing this book, starting from reviewing and editing the manuscript, followed by other technical matters, the publication of this book remains relevant because issues regarding family are issues of all time. By also passing the COVID-19 pandemic period during the process, it is hoped that the publication of this book will continue to provide contributions from a theoretical and practical perspective to the scientific world, especially psychology, in preparing the family as the most important place for the growth and development of individuals who will become part of the social structure of society.

Finally, the editorial team would like to express their deepest apologies and gratitude to all academics and researchers who have contributed to this book chapters, for their writing contributions and their patience in waiting for this book to be published. Hopefully this book can add to the scientific treasures of psychology, especially about the family and all its problems.

Marcus Stueck on behalf of Ami Zulaifah, Dian Utami (Book seria editors)

Foreword of the editors of the book seria

Family in Islamic and Western Perspectives - Biocentric Commonalities and Family Health

This volume deals with various research and reflections on the healthy family, especially in the Islamic context. A healthy family is characterised by many factors, all of which are interconnected and influence each other. For example, families play an important role in the transmission of values and norms, which are of great importance for the moral and ethical development of children, adolescents and parents. This, in turn, is linked to the development of violence-reduced and reflective behaviour among family members.

The book "Family in Islamic Psychology Perspective" is a collection of various scientific articles that examine and describe the above-mentioned factors of healthy families and its interconnection between the factors. It also increases the reflexion about the pathological parts, in different target groups. These articles are the result of a conference in Indonesia in 2019 on this topic. This book about "Family in Islamic Psychology Perspective" is volume 2 of the book series "Islamic Psychology and Biopsychological Basics of Life in Education and Health". Volume 1 is the book Islamic Psychology - An Integrative Dialogue Psychology, Spirituality, Science and Art. The aim of the book series and the books in it is to create a bridge in which knowledge from the so-called Islamic and the occidental, so-called Western world is exchanged and vice versa.

The book series "Islamic Psychology and Biopsychological Basics in Education and Helath" and its books enables readers in the Islamic world as well as in the Western world to develop an understanding for the other perspective, to broaden their own perspective and to enter into dialogue with each other. This approach of relative truths depending on the perspective has been scientifically described by the Biocentric Health Theory (Stueck, 2021). From the Islamic perspective, the following family values could be relevant.

1. sense of community: there is a strong sense of community in Islamic culture. Family members often share their lives and resources with each other.
2. Respect for elders: Islamic culture places great emphasis on respect for elders, especially parents and grandparents.

3. Family as a source of moral and ethical education: In Islamic culture, the family is often seen as a source of moral education. Parents are responsible for educating their children in moral and ethical values. Islamic culture places great emphasis on the family as a unit and emphasises the importance of mutual support, respect and care.
4. Family as a place of spiritual practise In Islamic families, people pray together or perform other spiritual practices together in the family. These rituals provide support and stabilise the family, especially in times of crisis.

From the Western perspective, what are some core characteristics of healthy families that can be observed and which can complement the Islamic perspective well?

1. Equality in the families: Western culture emphasises equality between men and women, especially in terms of education, work and family.
2. Openness in the communication in families: Western culture is often very open and communicative, also in the family. Family members talk openly about their feelings and problems and look for solutions together.
3. Individuality and personal freedom of the family members: Western culture emphasises individuality and personal freedom, especially with regard to personal decisions and life choices.
4. Acceptance of differences in the family: Western culture is often very open to different lifestyles and beliefs, even within the family. Family members accept each other and support each other even if they have different opinions and beliefs.

It is important to emphasise here that Western culture as well as the Islamic culture are very diverse and there are different traditions and practices in different countries and communities. It is therefore important to look at each culture individually and understand which specific teachings and values are most relevant to them.

This communication about and presentation of different perspectives is a biocentric value. There is no absolute truth about what a healthy family is. The truth is relative to the experience of the individuals, the family, the culture. The books which are published in this book-series "Islamic psychology and biopsychological basics in education and health" have a biocentric orientation. BIOS is life and centric, means that life is at the centre. Where there is life, love is not far away. The biocentric importance of the family lies primarily in its role as the primary source of emotional support, Love and intimate bonding with secure attachment patterns and relationships. Family members should offer each other love, safety, security and care, which contributes to children and adults experiencing healthy psychological development and having their emotional needs met.

Stueck (2021) describes the relationship to life and family in families in a biocentric health theory the following basic biocentric assumption:

> "Where there is life, there is love. The two are inseparable. The connection with life comes from the connection with love and vice versa. Life and the love connected to it are sacred and must be protected in the culture, in the work, in the family. When people are connected to life and love, in big and small ways, from childhood onwards in their families, then a non-violent culture is possible with a reduction of diseases, wars, disasters, exhaustion, loneliness. Where life and love are connected in the human being, chaos is transformed into order (1st Biocentric Preliminary Basic Assumption).

Toro (2004, 2005, 2010, Stueck, Villegas) described the role of the family in his biocentric principles, namely that through affective bonds with parents, through tender contact and protection, through shared experiences, children gain access to life and love in a culture of hope with life-affirming attitudes. The learning should be affection-based and experiential in balance to the cognitive learning. This book shows people ways to connect with life and love, something of enormous importance for the health of individuals, but also for families, large and small, and from childhood. Biocentric approach is a path of inclusion and of exclusion of affective pathologies: e.g. racism, de-evaluation of the others, inability to express emotions and to communicate verbaly and non-verbaly.

As the above examples show, both Islamic and Western families can develop various factors of healthy families together, also taking into account different cultural, religious, psychological perspectives. The following biocentric characteristics of healthy families in Islamic and Western cultures can be derived from the considerations:

Development of Loving and Respectful Communication in Families: Both Islamic and Western families can learn from respectful communication, where family members actively listen and respond to each other without judging or devaluing. Respectful communication helps to reduce conflict and improve understanding and bonding within the family.

Development of Flexibility: Both Islamic and Western families can learn to be flexible and adapt their traditional values and practices to meet the needs and preferences of their family members. Families should be willing to question their traditions and ideas and, if necessary, find new ways to achieve their goals and values.

Development of Collaboration: Both Islamic and Western families can learn from collaboration, where family members work together on projects or goals.

Collaboration promotes understanding and support between family members and helps resolve conflicts and find solutions.

Development of Present relationships with enough time: Both Islamic and Western families can learn from effective time management to have enough time and presence, awareness, for work, family, education, health and leisure activities. Related to the biocentric Health Theory (Stueck, 2021), the moment is the only place, where Life and the inseparable Love exist (biocentric basic assumption).

Development of Inclusiveness: Both Islamic and Western families can learn from an inclusive attitude that accepts and celebrates diversity and differences within the family. Families should strive to accept and respect their differences and value the unique qualities and abilities of each family member.

It is important to note that these points do not apply equally to all cultures and families and that each family must be considered individually. Nevertheless, these points can serve as a guide to promote cooperation and understanding between Islamic and Western families.

May the book "Family in Islamic Psychology Perspective" provide a reflective opportunity to think about one's own fmily and to learn about research that has examined families.

Literature

Stueck, M. (2021). The Pandemic Management Theory. COVID-19 and biocentric development. *Health Psychology Report*, pp. 101-128.

Stueck M.,Villegas A.(2019), Dance towards health? Empirical research to Biodanza- Biodanza mirrored in the science, Strasburg, Schibri

Toro, R. (2004). The biocentric principle. International Biocentric Foundation, Biodanzaschule Leipzig. Unpublished manuscript.

Toro, R. (2005). The biocentric education. Internation- al Biocentric Foundation, Biodanzaschule Leipzig. Unpublished manuscript.

Toro R. (2010), The Biodanza System (The dance of life), Hannover: Tinto

Acknowledgement

Praise and gratitude are only for Allah swt., Who knows all that is in the heavens and the earth. Knowledge of Allah swt. includes what is real and what is hidden, what has happened, is happening, or will happen. Blessings and peace may always be with the Prophet Muhammad SAW. The Prophet who in all matters could be a role model for his people, including in knowledge.

Thank God, this book about the family, after going through a long effort, can finally be published, and can be enjoyed by the wider community. This is of course a great joy for the Faculty of Psychology UIN Sunan Gunung Djati Bandung, the editors, and the writers. Happiness for higher education institutions and researchers when their scientific products are published and have a positive impact on society. As gratitude for the publication of this anthology, we would like to thank

1. Rector of UIN Sunan Gunung Djati, Prof. Dr. Mahmud, M.Sc, who always encourages the Faculty to carry out quality activities and have a positive impact on society
2. Dean of the Faculty of Cultural Sciences and Psychology, Indonesian Islamic University, Dr. Fuad Nashori, M.Sc, who is pleased to collaborate with scientific publications and facilitate communication with publishers.
3. International Institute of Islamic Thought (IIIT) represented by Dr. M. Habib Chirzin who is willing to collaborate and facilitate the presence of speakers from abroad
4. Marcus Stueck and publisher Peter Lang helped with the publication of this book.
5. The technical team for compiling the anthology book led by Dr. Rosleny Marliani, M.Sc, who for a long time supervised the process of publishing this book.
6. Writers from various universities, who have entrusted their research results to be published in this book, and are waiting patiently for the publication process

We pray that the hard work and contribution of the parties mentioned above will be accepted by Allah swt. as goodness and gain His pleasure. Amen

Table of Contents

Marcus Stueck[1] and Nur'aini Azizah[2]

Introduction

International Biocentric Research Academy Leipzig[1]
Universitas Islam Negeri Sunan Gunung Djati Bandung, Indonesia [2]

The family is an important source of social support and assistance during times of crisis. After the COVID 19 crisis, many family issues emerged that suddenly became important. For example, the parent-child relationship, conflict resolution, maternal and paternal parenting styles, coping with illness and difficulties. Especially in times of illness, unemployment, or other difficulties, family members can help and support each other, which can help them cope with challenging situations more effectively. The family is also an important institution for social integration by bringing together members of different generations, genders, and cultural backgrounds, and providing them with opportunities to share common experiences and learn from one another. This can help promote understanding and tolerance of others and strengthen social cohesion. Overall, the family is a crucial component of human life and has profound importance for individual and collective well-being and social development and the development of the character of children.

The discussion in the first book chapter starts with the theme of the role of the family in strengthening children's character in the technological era. The family has a very fundamental role in helping to stimulate the good character of children, especially in providing good basic education in accordance with applicable regulations. The family qualitatively becomes the initial gate for the formation of a child's good character, so it is important for the community to explore the roles of parents and their relationship with children.

The second chapter explains the role of religious coping and the perception of self-acceptance of the anxiety that arises in pregnant women. This second chapter presents a quantitative design which provides quite complete information about the things that a mother must prepare in preparing for the smooth running of their labour. The facts show that the positive aspect of religiosity in a wife can contribute to reducing their pregnancy anxiety.

In the next chapter, the authors present a quantitative study that is almost the same as the previous one, which places the power of spirituality as an important variable in determining adolescent Well-Being. Specifically, the interesting thing about this research is that it is their subjects who experience juvenile delinquency. The results of the research contribute to the formation of family social support and spirituality as an important factor for adolescents to perform optimally.

Entering the fourth chapter, the discussion goes into families who have special children or with special needs. Packed with a unique qualitative research design, this research strengthens readers about the importance of wisdom and knowledge in families who have children with special needs. Even though they have many limitations, it is possible that children with special needs have a myriad of extraordinary potentials that can be developed through a good family. This is the uniqueness of the research in this chapter

In chapter 5, the authors present a quantitative study conducted on mothers who have children with cerebral palsy. The uniqueness of the subjects in this study is very important to identify considering that it will provide in-depth information about the importance of character strength in a mother. Mothers with all the strength they have are required to have optimism and family resilience in raising their children.

Chapter 6 is discussing how the role of the family in shaping the character of a child. Unlike the previous characteristics of children, studies on children are focused on their tolerant behavior which will be very important to develop in childhood. In general, there are two factors that influence children's behavior, namely the involvement of children and parents and self-regulation.

Furthermore, in chapter 7, the authors provide information regarding the role of the family in other aspects for individuals. The design used is quantitative with many samples so that it can be an advantage in this study. What's interesting is that the results of this study show that the social anxiety experienced by a teenager is largely determined by his closeness to his parents and the strengthening of the adolescent's own identity. The practical implications of the research results provide quite a lot of information for the clinical development of adolescents.

In chapter 8, the authors are discussing how the developmental stages of children at a young age will greatly impact their growth. Just like other sections that emphasize the role of the family in child development, this section also states that intense positive parenting given to children will strengthen their readiness when entering school. This is of course valuable information for parents as an initial strategy for their child's success in school

The authors in chapter 9 explain the importance of character education for individuals to face their social life. In difficult and uncertain times like this, strengthening self-identity is important so that they don't easily fall into a bad environment. As also explained in this chapter about the importance of character education

In chapter 10, there is an interesting method used by researchers in explaining resilience issues from an Islamic perspective. With the thematic content analysis research model, the researcher can produce a description explaining activities and rituals in building family resilience based on an Islamic perspective. This is a quite unique study because it emphasizes the strength of the method in the study of Islamic literature.

In chapter 11, the authors conduct research related to innovative solutions regarding cases of divorce and healthy marriages. This research examines the effectiveness of Islamic premarital education to increase marriage readiness. With a repeated measurement design research model involving 16 unmarried young adults. With a range of 19-31 years. The finding shows that there are differences in marriage readiness created by Islamic premarital education that have a large and substantive effect on increasing readiness for new adult marriage in Indonesia.

Chapter 12 discusses the relationship between family and technology. In the Digital Age, technology plays an important role in everyday life. Most human activities depend on technology, such as working, studying, and even preparing food. A survey conducted by the Association of Indonesian Internet Service Providers (APJII) in collaboration with technopreneurs in 2017 found that in Indonesia there were 143.26 million internet users, including children. Through psychoeducation, parents will also learn new life skills to educate and equip their children to face the impacts of the digital era, especially excessive internet use. This research uses one group post test design with descriptive analysis. Based on these results, participants demonstrated a better understanding of the effects of excessive internet use and how to positively guide their children.

Chapter 13 examines whether self-efficacy and social support influence craving, both simultaneously and separately. The design of this study uses the correlational causality method, while the data collection uses a questionnaire. The sample used in this study was 40 clients at the Pamardi Putri Social Institution Galih Pakuan Bogor who had gone through 3 stages to be declared cured of drug abuse. It can be concluded that self-efficacy and social support have a simultaneous influence on the craving of drug users at the Pamardi Putra Panti. Social support especially from the family is needed by clients during the therapy period.

Chapter 14 examine the correlation between the husband's self-concept and infidelity. The result show that t F test in show a significance value of. 392>. 05. Therefore, it can be concluded that there is no significant relationship between self-concept and husband's infidelity. the value of R square is. 024, so that the role of self-concept on husband's infidelity is 2.4% and 97.6% is related to other factors. In conclusion that they have a positive self-image, namely believing that as husbands they are good husbands, loyal and reliable by their wives, and feel satisfied with themselves.

In chapter 15, authors used a qualitative approach with data collection techniques in the form of observation and interviews. The participants in this study were 10 teenagers who lived and were active in Bandung and had committed naughty acts. In addition, researchers also interviewed 5 members of youth organizations who are active in preventing juvenile delinquency. The results of this study indicate that juvenile delinquency that occurs in Cipadung village can be categorized into 1. Acts that cause physical victims to others, 2. Delinquency that does not cause victims to others, and 3. Delinquency against status. To tackle juvenile delinquency, the BRC (Blocking Radicalism Community) plays an important role in reducing and preventing juvenile delinquency.

By using the IPA method, Chapter 16 explores about father's understanding on his function as a father because of the parenting style applied to them as well as the religious point of view. In applying to become a father, respondents stated that they applied the mindset "I can be a father" when facing obstacles faced in becoming a father. Apart from that, the two respondents also instilled the belief that no matter how little time they had, they should be able to meet and get along with their children. Finally, both respondents acknowledged that the wife has an important role in imparting fatherly values to their children.

Neng Gustini[1], Heny Mulyani[2], and Asep Encu[3]

Strengthening Children's Honest Character in Millennial Families

Universitas islam Negeri Sunan Gunung Djati Bandung, Indonesia[1]
Indonesian University of Education, Indonesia[2]
Indonesian University of Education, Indonesia[3]

Abstract. This study aims to describe the role of parents in millennial families in strengthening honest character to their children. Industrial Revolution 4.0 as the global trend of digital technology gives significant changes to human life and society. The moral and character building in early childhood is essential to encounter this challenge. This character building begins from the smallest unit in the society which is family. The data in this study were analyzed using descriptive qualitative analysis. The observation object of this study is parents of Madrasah Ibtidaiyah (MI) An-Na'iim students. The results of the study indicate that the strategies applied by the parents in strengthening honest character are giving good examples, giving advice, open communication, discussion, involving proportionally in children's activities, giving understanding and awareness, and communicating the importance of having honest character through reading stories.

Keywords: Millennial, family, honest character

1 Introduction

Family is a social system with various social behaviors that are different and belong to each individual in the family. A complete family consists of a father, a mother, and children. Family has a very important role in forming an individual's character and personality because family is the first and foremost place of education for children. Therefore, the good and bad moral of a nation will depend on how education is applied in the family. If individuals grow and live in a harmonious family, they will create a good generation. On the contrary, if there are frequent quarrels in the family, it will create a fragile generation. Parents in millennial families are born in the early 1980s to the 2000s. The children in millennial families are born in the era of information and technological advances. They enjoy various facilities and easy access to information, transportation, and other modern technologies. This generation is very protective, confident, team-oriented, prestigious, and prone to depression (Neil Howe & William Strauss, 2003). In the digital era, the millennial families tend to use technology as a tool to support their daily activities, such as using smartphone to communicate between family members. The smartphone is also used to access the latest information from around the world. The families with such characteristics are known as the Millennial Generation Family. This condition creates challenges for the millennial families including the rise of pornography in the cyberspace, easy access to criminal acts information that may be imitated and affect the development of family members (Rahardian, 2015).

Nowadays, there has been a decline in children's character and mental health. Criminal act is massive, and based on the data from the National Police Headquarters, there has been an increase in criminality committed by the millennial youth from 2007 to 2009. In many cases, millennials who commit misbehavior acts lead to social deviations that violate regulations and even commit a crime. Those acts include consuming alcohol, reckless driving, consuming drugs, theft, fraud, rape, fights, murder, and so forth (Agung Wiradimadja, 2019). Thus, it is clear that this digital era or technology development can affect family life, both positively and negatively. The positive side is that we easily access and communicate with other people, open wide horizons, and get knowledge easily. The negative side is that it can influence individual's moral and character development in the family, and it can influence interaction patterns within the family. Furthermore, various social media applications and online games can also interfere interaction and communication patterns within the family because each family member is active in accessing social media or online games, so it can cause misunderstandings or misperceptions among family members (Sapty, 2012).

These cases indicate the non-functioning role of the family as an institution and the role of parents in shaping the children's character. The gaps of the economic conditions in the community and correlation of current parenting pattern with previous generation parenting pattern are the factors that weaken character and mentality of the millennial generation. Parents in the previous generations educated their children a little bit hard. Cultural values and norms are the benchmarks in character building. Therefore, a family needs to maintain family values and functions by cultivating moral and character education in the family. Since a family is part of society, early childhood character education is the responsibility of all elements of society. Character education can be done from early childhood through daily habituation (Haira, 2018). Character is very essential for living, so it must be well formed in order to create a safe, orderly, and prosperous society. Ratna Megawangi (2004, p. 1) adds that the demoralization in society will give a negative impact on civilization. Civilized communities are built from strong families by investing education and values towards their members. One of the most important characters in children is honest character.

Honesty will make someone easy to achieve success, to have many friends, and to be confident. Honesty is a self-reflection that may measure how much is our life quality. This opinion is in line with Sunaryo's (2012) argument. He says that honest individuals will have advantages, including a calm life because they don't need to think about problems arising from their lies, and have many friends and good reputation. Honest individuals will get success because honesty is one of basic principles to achieve success. The emphasis on the importance of the honest character should give a good impact and influence on society. A research conducted by western psychologists supports Prophet Muhammad PBUH's argument that honesty brings goodness, happiness, and success in the world and the afterlife. Anita E. Kelly (2012, as cited in Suud, 2017 & Haira, 2018) also proves that participants had improvement in health such as experiencing less headaches, less sore throat, and less anxiety. In addition to a better health, the participants who do not tell lies also improved interpersonal relationships with the others. Furthermore, the Hadith clearly states that the inventions brought on honesty and kindness could bring someone to heaven.

Based on a preliminary study in December 2018 at Madrasah Ibtidaiyah Bandung Regency, the elementary students, who were not used to being honest, were not willing to admit when they made mistakes. Such children were also difficult to accept the superiority of others, and had a tendency to steal other's belonging. These conditions show that education has not succeeded in cultivating honest character in children. Therefore, it is important to strengthen honest character in children from an early age, especially in the era of Industrial Revolution 4.0 when there is a widespread of lies/hoaxes in cyberspace. As revealed by Schiller (cited in Yaumi, 2014, p. 65), only with honesty, we can have a better direction in living, and without honesty, we will experience setback in our civilization. Unfortunately, the studies related to the impact of Industrial Revolution 4.0 on the family, especially about cultivating character, is still very minimal. This shows that family development is still not a strategic issue recently. Thus, what is the role of the millennial family in maintaining its function to ensure the building of honest character in children?

2 Literature Review

2.1 Role of Millennial Family in the Industrial Revolution 4.0

Families have a major role in nurturing and educating children, with all norms and ethics that apply in the community. Parent has a primary role in teaching their children, considering the role of parent as *madrasah al-ula* (Dwi Hayantina

Sunarni, 2018). A family carries out its role as a social system that can shape the children's character. This opinion is in line with the resolution of the general assembly of the United Nations (Megawangi, 2004) that the main function of the family is to be a medium for educating, nurturing, and socializing children, developing all members' ability to carry out their functions well in society, and providing satisfaction and healthy environment in order to achieve a prosperous family. The Industrial Revolution 4.0 has tremendous potential in changing industrial aspects and human life, and it starts from the state affairs of a nation. However, the Industrial Revolution 4.0 needs to be supported by ecosystems with advanced human resources who are adaptive to technology developments. In fact, unwittingly the presence of Industrial Revolution 4.0 has shaped family behavior, especially in parenting including the rights, obligations, responsibilities, and development of roles both inside and outside the home. This opinion is in line with Karen's argument that we must understand the impact of Industrial Revolution 4.0 on families, especially among the millennial generation. Millennials are born between 1981and 2000, and they are now (2006) aged six years to 25 years (Neil Howe & William Strauss, 2003). In fact, the data show that more than half of Millennials have at least college education (54%), compared to 49% of Gen Xers, 36% of Boomers, and 24% of the Silent generation when they were in ages of 18 to 28. Millennials are more highly educated than other generations at comparable ages www.pewresearch.org/millennials. This condition indicates that highly educated millennial family will be settled in educating their children.

2.2 Character Education, Honest Character, and Influencing Aspects and Factors

Ki Hajar Dewantara said that character education is the most important subject given to children in early age. The parents should build values, human dignity, moral values, character, and human personality—kind acts to regulate human life. The person will be a good and honorable human being, if he invested the five attitudes and behavior (Sujiono, 2014, as cited in Haira, 2018).

Etymologically, the character is derived from *Charassein* (the Greek language), which means carving so that a pattern is formed (Bohlin, 2001). Education experts explain that the formation of individual characters is determined by nature factors (natural; *fitrah*) and nurture factors (socialization and education). The nature factors (or *fitrah*) means that humans have *fitrah* (tendency) to do goodness. However, if it is not followed by a nurturing factor (education and socialization), humans may behave like animals or even worse (Brooks, David, & Goble, 1997). Meanwhile, for honesty, Tara Tomczyk K. (2009, p. 27) explains that being honest means telling the truth and behaving respectably, including do not lie, cheat, or steal, saying the facts, avoiding bias or exaggeration, and bending the truth even if it will benefit you. Honest people not only behave honestly with others but also themselves.

Tara Tomczyk K. (2009, pp. 27–32) explains that honesty has many forms, including academic honesty, integrity, sincerity, scientific honesty, honor, trust, and sportsmanship. Honesty consists of three parts which are (a) true honesty with faith, (b) true intentions in speech, (c) words that are true in speech (Ibn Qayyim al-Jauzi, 1999, p. 399). This opinion is supported by Said Hawa (2007, pp. 322–328) that honest consists of six aspects, including (1) honest in words (telling), (2) honest in intention and willing, (3) honest in *'Azam* (determination), (4) honest in keeping determination, (5) honest in deeds (working /*'amal*), and (6) honest in various religious services, such *as shidiq in khauf, raja ', ta'zhim, zuhud,* happy, *tawakkal,* love, and so on. There are three factors that influence honest character. First factor is family factor. It is important to develop honest character in early childhood. It can begin with habituation by parents at home. Second factor is motivation. There are internal and external motivations. External motivation can be applied by giving awards. For example, a child who is honest will be given a compliment or gift so that there is a reinforcement in doing honest actions (Dwijatmoko, Benedictus Bherman). The last factor is social and cultural factors, including social position, intimacy, and facing threats, and norms of work and life (Dwijatmoko, Benedictus Bherman, 2018).

3 Method

This study uses a qualitative approach with descriptive methods. This study aims to obtain information about strengthening honest character in millennial families who have primary school-age children in Bandung Regency. The data was reduced, interpreted, and analyzed to find out its meaning and presented in a narrative and descriptive manner.

3.1 Sample

The research respondents were determined by a purposive sample technique. The selected participants in the study were families who were married between 1990 and 2017 and had children in elementary school (grades 1–6). This limitation on respondents was made based on the purpose of the study to examine parenting conducted by millennial parent generation. The number of interviewed respondents was 30 families. These families were scattered in Bandung Regency.

3.2 Measurement Tools

The data collection was done through interviews. It was done by semi-structured interviews in order to get in-depth information from the respondents. Interview guidelines were designed specifically to get information on what efforts have been made by the parents to add insight within their parenting. Data were taken from interviews based on interview guidelines that had been prepared, the distributed to interviewees and the results were reduce and analyzed by collaboration with results of other studies. Data analysis techniques included data collection, data reduction, presentation of data (data displays), and conclusions.

4 Results

Based on the data obtained through the interview, in strengthening honesty to children, parenting was dominated by mothers who mostly are housewives. The data obtained from interviews with parents of students of MI An-Na'iim Bandung Regency shows that mothers have more active roles than fathers in cultivating honest character by making programs and activities which trigger openness and communication, such as on time prayers, deep-talk, giving trust to children, reading stories about honesty, and other programs that were followed by children enthusiastically.

4.1 Discussion

Based on the findings above on the general description of family role in strengthening honest character, it can be understood that mothers have more active roles than fathers. Meanwhile, in the families whose parents are entrepreneurs and civil servants, fathers' and mothers' roles are not significantly different in cultivating honest character in their children. The result concerning the role of parents (family) in cultivating honest character is in line with the research conducted by Nenci Permatasari (2016) about parents' role in developing children's characters. It was found that giving examples was used in teaching honest character. This is similar to Kurniawan's argument (2013, p. 86) that honesty in adulthood is inseparable from honesty cultivated by family/parents when they are young (early age). Thus, parents must become the role models for their children in cultivating honest character by improving parenting quality through open communication between parents and children. As a result, the parents will understand the basic needs of children, both physically and emotionally. In addition, parents should not lie to their children and respect children's honesty. According to Stats and Hagley (2008, as cited in Suud, 2017 & Haira, 2018), the student's honesty could be improved through the development of courage and empathy. NIKMAH ROCHMAWATI (2018) adds that the role of parents (families) in cultivating honest character in the millennial era could be done through (1) raising awareness that lying is dangerous and emphasizing the importance of being honest in life, (2) don't be ashamed to ask forgiveness if parents do something wrong and/or forget the promises they made, (3) answering the children's questions correctly according to the stage of development, (4) giving sufficient attention and supervision to the children, (5) reading stories about honest character then discuss it with them, telling examples of honest and dishonest behaviors, and maintaining an honest friend, and (6) applying honest character when playing, learning, interacting with parents, friends, teachers, siblings, and older people by respecting children's honesty. For example, parents can say "thank you, kid, you're honest." In addition, Ki Hajar Dewantara says that human development, especially child development, is divided into several age intervals which are (1) childhood, about 1–7 years old in which giving examples and habituation are the appropriate education at this stage and (2) a growth period of soul and mind about 7–14 years old in which appropriate education is done through learning, commanding, or punishing (Sujiono, 2014 as cited in Haira, 2018). This Research has some limitations in which the subject of research was limited, and the use of descriptive method with the interview was done without observation as a measurement tool. Therefore, it is expected that the research in the future will have a wider subject and scope by using quantitative data. It may test the effective formulas and models to cultivate honest character or other good characters in children.

5 Conclusion

Based on data obtained through surveys and interviews, it can be concluded that the role of millennial families in cultivating the children's honest character in the era of Industrial Revolution 4.0 requires the role of both parents, father and mother, in the same proportion. Cultivating honest character in children at the early age can be done through giving a good example, applying honest character under any conditions and to anyone, open communication, good quality discussions and involvement within children's activities, providing understanding, raising awareness, and emphasizing the importance of being honest with children and telling the consequences of dishonesty through reading stories about honest characters.

6 Affiliations

1. Name:	Neng Gustini
Institution:	Universitas Islam Negeri Sunan Gunung Djati Bandung, Indonesia
Address:	Jl. Dr. Setiabudhi No 229, Jl. AH. Nasution No 108
E-mail:	gustine1981@gmail.com, neng.gustini@uinsdg.ac.id,

2. Name:	Heny Mulyani
Institution:	UIN Sunan Gunung Djati Bandung, Indonesia,
Address:	Jl. Cimincrang Gedebage, Bandung
Email:	henymulyani@uinsgd.ac.id

3. Name:	Asep Encu
Institution::	UIN Sunan Gunung Djati Bandung, Indonesia,
Address::	Jl. Cimincrang Gedebage, Bandung,
E-mail:	asepencu1963@gmail.com

7 References

Bohlin, Karen, et al. (2001). Building Character in Schools: Resource Guide. California: Jossey-Bass.

Brooks, David, & Goble. (1997). The Case for Character Education: The Role of the School in Teaching Values and Virtue. California: Studio 4.

Cohn, D' Vera. (2010). Downloaded from:www.pewresearch.org/millennials on February 2nd, 2020.

Dwijatmoko, Benedictus Bherman. (2018). Honesty in Indonesian Literature: Its Social and Cultural Factors. *Journal of Language Studies, 18*(4): 95–105.

Hawa, Said. (2007). Purifying the Soul. Jakarta: Rabbani Press.

Howe, Neil, & Strauss, William. (2003). Millennials Go to College. Retrieved: www.livecourse.com

Haira, Yuhasriati. (2018). Strengthening the Honesty Character of Young Children at the Islamic Integrated Preschool of MON Kuta Banda Aceh. Proceedings of the International Conference on the Roles of Parents in Shaping Children's Characters (ICECED), 46–49.

Kurniawan, Syamsul. (2013). Character Building. Yogyakarta: Ar-Ruzz Media.

K., Tara Tomczyk,. (2009). Character Education: Being Fair and Honest. New York: Chelsea House Publisher.

Megawangi, Ratna. (2004). Character Building. Jakarta: BP Migas & Star Energi.

Permatasari, Nenci. (2016). The Role of Parents in Shaping Children's Character in the City of Padang. Padang: STKIP PGRI West Sumatra.

Rahardian, Elfan, J. (2015). Utilization of the Internet and Its Impact on High School Students in Surabaya. Surabaya: Department of Information and Libraries, Faculty of Social and Political Sciences, Airlangga University.

Rochmawati, Nikmah. (2018). The Role of Teachers and Parents Shaping Honest Character in Children. *Al-Fikri Journal of Islamic Education Studies and Research, 1*(2).

Sapty, Flourensia, R. (2012). Cyberbullying as a Negative Impact of the Use of Information Technology. Yogyakarta: Atma Jaya Yogyakarta University.

Sunaryo, K. (2012). Benefits of Honesty. Download from: http irenetereisia.blogspot.co.id.

Sunarni, Dwi Hayantina. (2018). The Parent Role in Early Childhood Character Building. *Journal of Empowerment*, 7 (2), 319–327.

Wiradimadja, Agung. (2019). Parenting Education: Building Characters and Holding in Millennial Mental Problems. *International Conference on Social Studies and Environmental Issues. Advances in Social Science, Education and Humanities Research*, 404, 146–149.

Yang benar Qayyim al- Jauzi, Ibn. (1999). Madaarijussalikin. Beirut: Dar al- Fikr.

Yaumi, Muhammad. (2014). Character Education: Foundation, Pillars, and Implementation. Jakarta: Prenadamedia Group.

Agus Abdul Rahman, Ida Tresna, Rosleny Marliani, and Ulfiah

Role of Religious Coping and Perceived Risk on Childbirth-Related Anxiety in Primigravidas

Universitas Islam Negeri Sunan Gunung Djati Bandung, Indonesia

Abstract. For women who are pregnant for the first time (*primigravidas*), dealing with childbirth is often very anxious. If this anxiety is not properly controlled, it will disturb and even endanger the delivery process. There are many factors that may help primigravidas to be calmer in dealing with childbirth such as primigravidas' perceptions on the childbirth risks and how primigravidas apply religious values in coping with their anxiety. The results of this study show that religious coping has a significant role in reducing childbirth-related anxiety, β = -.276 and p =. 020. On the other hand, the perceived risk increases childbirth-related anxiety, β =. 392 and p =. 013. In addition, religious coping and perceived risk collectively have a significant effect on childbirth-related anxiety in primigravidas with F= 3.21 and p =. 003, and value of R^2 =. 237. In addition, the results of this study show that religious coping has a significant role to reduce childbirth-related anxiety, β = -.276 and p =. 020, while perceived risk has a role in increasing childbirth-related anxiety, β =. 392 and p =. 013. In addition, religious coping and perceived risk collectively have a significant effect on childbirth-related anxiety in primigravidas with F= 3.21, p =. 003 and R^2 =. 237. Religious coping and perceived risk have an effect of 23.7% on childbirth-related anxiety. It can be implied that in order to reduce primigravidas' anxiety, primigravidas' perceptions on childbirth risk shall widen, and they may apply religious values in coping with their anxiety.

Keywords: Religious coping, perceived risk, childbirth-related anxiety, primigravidas, pregnant women

1 Introduction

Pregnancy is the most beautiful gift for a family, especially for a woman who is pregnant for the first time (*primigravida*). The first pregnancy is a new phase in a woman's life. It has a deep meaning, and it gives a lot of happiness and hope. For primigravidas, despite of the happiness, pregnancy makes them anxious and afraid (Kartono, 2007).

Anxiety is an emotional state characterized by physiological arousal, unpleasant feeling, and apprehensive feeling (a state of fearful) about bad things that will happen to them (Nevid, Spencer, & Ruthus, 2005). In fact, the anxiety and fear are unavoidable. The anxiety usually gets worse in near time of childbirth. Primigravida feels worried, anxious, afraid, uncertain, and overthinking about her pregnancy condition as well as her future duties as a mother . According to Sarifah's research (2016), among 40 respondents, there was no primigravida who had a normal anxiety level. The research showed that 9 women had mild anxiety, 12 women had moderate anxiety, 11 women had severe anxiety, and 8 women had very severe anxiety. This result is in line with a research conducted by Usman, Kundre, and Onibala (2016) with 61 respondents. Their research showed that 41 respondents experienced severe anxiety, 13 respondents experienced moderate anxiety, and 6 respondents experienced mild anxiety during their first pregnancy. Only 1 respondent did not experience anxiety. From the data, it can be seen that the primigravidas' anxiety when facing childbirth is quite high.

The preliminary research conducted by the researcher on April 8, 2017, showed that among the 10 primigravidas interviewed by the researcher, 3 women experienced mild anxiety, 3 women experienced moderate anxiety, 2 women experienced severe anxiety and 2 women have low anxiety. Such anxiety was generally caused by negative perception on childbirth. They perceived that the process of giving birth for the first time would be painful and would take a long time. They were also worried about the baby's health, childbirth cost, possibility of caesarean delivery, etc.

Anxiety issue during pregnancy should get serious attention from local governments, doctors, and researchers. Uncontrolled anxiety will lead to abnormal delivery such as premature birth and prolonged labor , excessive nausea and vomiting (*hiperemesis gravidarum*), increased high blood pressure (pre-eclampsia), and even seizures in women who have pre-eclampsia. In addition, mothers who experience anxiety in childbirth may cause low APGAR score to the babies, physical and mental health problems to the mothers and the babies, an increased probability of postpartum depression to the mothers, and low body weight of the babies (Yang benar adalah Aryani, Raden, & Ismarwati, 2017). Sarifah (2016) adds that anxiety can make the mothers feel more pain during the delivery.

2 Literature Review

Anxiety is an emotional state characterized by physiological arousal, unpleasant feeling, and apprehensive feeling (a state of fearful) about bad things that will happen to them (Yang benar: Nevid, Rathus, & Greene, 2005 Nevid, Spencer, & Ruthus, 2005). Kaplan, Sadock, and Grebb (1994) define anxiety as a response to a certain threatening situation, and it is a normal condition that accompanies developments, changes, new experiences, or any event that has not been experienced by a person as well as any process of finding self-identity and meaning in life.

Childbirth-related anxiety is similar to an anxiety in general, but it is specifically related to the emotional state felt by a pregnant woman in the form of worries and fear for baby's health, delivery process, health experience in hospital, childbirth and postpartum, and her roles and responsibilities as a mother .

According to Adler and Rodman (1991), there are two factors that cause anxiety which are (a) a negative experience in the past which may happen again in the future and (b) irrational thoughts. Kartono (2007) explains some factors that may influence anxiety, fear, and worry before childbirth, including fear of death, birth trauma, guilty feeling, and real fear. On the other hand, Zenden, et al. (1985, in Mahmudah, 2010) argue that some factors affecting the anxiety before childbirth are marital status, socioeconomic status, knowledge level of pregnant women, social support, sincerity, and trust in God.

Negative thoughts about perceived risks are presumed to contribute to the anxiety in facing the delivery process. Slovic (2000) explains that perceived risk is a subjective judgment and interpretation made by an individual on threatening events, while Sjober, Moen, and Rundmo (2004, in Lifshitz, Nimrod, & Bachner, 2016) argue that perceived risk is a subjective judgment on the possibility of difficulties and how an individual deals with and feels about the consequences.

Slovic (2000, in Peak & Hove, 2017) explains that there are two main elements of perceived risk, namely cognitive and emotional dimensions. The cognitive dimension is related to the individual's ability to know and understand the risk to be faced. On the other hand, emotional dimension is related to the individual's feelings about the risk. According to Kusmawati (2006), some risks that may affect the perceived risk of pregnant women in the delivery process are maternal factors, nutritional factors, health factors, pregnancy check-up factors, and delivery assistance.

Negative thoughts sometimes are unavoidable, especially for a primigravida who is exposed with a high risk due to pregnancy. Therefore, it is necessary to minimize the influence of such negative thoughts so that the anxiety in childbirth is not too high. One of the factors that may help to reduce the anxiety is religious values. Thus, this study examines the role of religious coping in moderating the relationship between the effect of perceived risk and childbirth-related anxiety.

According to Pargament, Feuille, & Burdzy (2011), religious coping is a method for understanding and dealing with stresses in life through a religious approach, whereas according to Koening (1998, in Reza, 2015), religious coping is the use of religious beliefs and ritual practices to prevent or alleviate psychological pressure from stressful situations. Pargament, Ensing, Harrison, and Koening (in Nelson, 2009) divide the religious coping styles into two: positive religious coping and negative religious coping. Positive religious coping involves a positive focus on problem solving through the religious dimension. Negative religious coping involves feeling of spiritual dissatisfaction and lack of expert support. Pargament, Koening, and Perez in 2000 classify religious coping into five dimensions, namely: (1) finding meaning; (2) self-control; (3) comfort and closeness to God: (4) having a close relationship with other people and God; (5) creating changes in life.

3 Method

This study employs a quantitative approach with a predictive relationship research design. This is used to predict a variable using other variables. In this approach, one variable has a role in predicting changes in another variable, and another variable is a variable whose changes are predicted (Rahman, 2016)

3.1 Sample

The sample in this study is 47 pregnant women who are primigravidas (having the first child), and their pregnancies are examined in Sumedang Regional General Hospital (RSUD). Since the population in this study is less than 100, all samples are observed. The composition of the population are 6 pregnant women in the second trimester of pregnancy and 41 pregnant women in the third trimester of pregnancy.

3.2 Measurement Tools

The data was collected from primigravidas by distributing a measuring instrument in the form of questionnaires about religious coping, perceived risk, and childbirth-related anxiety. The primigravidas had to respond to each item in the questionnaire.

3.2.1 Religious Coping Scale

Based on The RCOPE adapted from Pargament, Feuille, & Burdzy (2011), religious coping is divided into five dimensions, namely meaning, control, comfort in spirituality, intimacy inspirituality, and life transformation. The religious coping scale consists of 44 items. The respondents who get a high score are considered to have a high religious level, and *vice versa*.

3.2.2 *Perceived Risk Scale*

Perceive Risk Scale is measured by a scale created by the researcher which consists of one aspect, namely cognitive. Such a scale is adopted from a measuring instrument made by Weber in 2002. Perceived risk scale consists of 18 items. The respondents who have a high score are considered to have high perceived risk, and *vice versa*.

3.2.3 *Childbirth-Related Anxiety Scale*

Anxiety scale is made by the researcher based on Sue's theory (2010) which consists of four dimensions, namely cognitive, affective, motoric and somatic. The childbirth-related anxiety scale consists of 35 items. The respondents who get a high score are considered to have a high level of childbirth-related anxiety.

3.3 Data Analysis

The research hypothesis was analyzed using multiple regression to predict the criterion variable which was childbirth-related anxiety, and predictor variables namely religious coping and perceived risk.

4 Results

Correlation analysis among the variables shows that the correlation between religious coping and childbirth-related anxiety is significant negative r_{person} = -.348, p =. 016. In addition, perceived risk and childbirth-related anxiety show a significant positive relationship with r_{person} =. 369, p =.011. In contrast, religious coping and perceived risk have no significant relationship, r_{person} = -.084 and p =.574. These results are in line with researcher's hypothesis as aforementioned. Further analysis shows that the effect of religious coping and perceived risk on childbirth-related anxiety is proved to be significant, F = 6.844 and p =. 003, R^2=.237 (23.7%). It is implied that religious coping and perceived risk are able to explain or influence childbirth-related anxiety in primigravidas by 23.7%. The rest of it (76.3%) can be explained or influenced by other variables.

Further, the relation of religious coping and childbirth-related anxiety has a regression coefficient of -.276 with p =. 020. It shows that p value is smaller than α value, which are. 020 <. 05. It means that there is a negative effect in the relation of religious coping and childbirth-related anxiety in primigravidas. Such result indicates that religious coping and childbirth-related anxiety are inversely proportional, so religious coping plays a role in reducing childbirth-related anxiety. If the primigravidas have a high religious coping, the level of childbirth-related anxiety will be low, and *vice versa*. This is in line with Pargament's and Barnt's (2000, in Gamayanti, 2012) research suggesting that one of the ways to solve individual problems is religious coping. In addition, the result is also in line with a research conducted by Reza (2016) stating that religious coping can overcome psychological problems in patients with kidney failure.

The relation of perceived risk and childbirth-related anxiety has a regression coefficient of. 392 with p =. 013. It shows that p value is smaller than α value, which is. 013 <. 05. It means that there is a positive effect in the relation of perceived risk and childbirth-related anxiety for primigravidas. Therefore, it can be implied that perceived risk is directly proportional to the childbirth-related anxiety, so the perceived risk may increase anxiety scores when primigravidas deal with childbirth. In other words, if primigravidas have a high perceived risk, the anxiety level in dealing with childbirth will be high, and *vice versa*. This is in line with Arini's (2012) argument that anxiety is closely related to perceived risk because anxiety appears when an individual feels in danger or faces a dangerous event.

5 Conclusions

The conclusions of this study shall be as follows:

7. Collectively, religious coping and perceived risk have an effect on childbirth-related anxiety in primigravidas, and are able to explain or influence the childbirth-related anxiety in primigravidas by 23.7%.
8. There is a negative effect in the relation of religious coping and childbirth-related anxiety in primigravidas. Religious coping may reduce childbirth-related anxiety. On the other hand, perceived risk has a positive effect on childbirth-related anxiety in primigravidas, and the perceived risk may increase childbirth-related anxiety.
9. It is predicted that childbirth-related anxiety will be reduced by increasing religious coping, and childbirth-related anxiety will be raised by the increase of perceived risk.

6 Affiliations

1. Name: Agus Abdul Rahman
Institution: UIN Sunan Gunung Djati Bandung
Address: Jln. A.H. Nasution No 105 Kota Bandung
E-mail: agus.abdulrahman@uinsgd.ac.id

2. Name: Ida Tresna
Institution: UIN Sunan Gunung Djati Bandung
Address: Jln. A.H. Nasution No 105 Kota Bandung
E-mail: idatresna24@gmail.com

3. Name: Rosleny Marliani
Institution: UIN Sunan Gunung Djati Bandung
Address: Jln. A.H. Nasution No 105 Kota Bandung
E-mail: roslenymarliani@uinsgd.ac.id

4. Name: Ulfiah
Institution: UIN Sunan Gunung Djati Bandung
Address: Jln. A.H. Nasution No 105 Kota Bandung
E-mail: ulfiah@uinsgd.ac.id

7 References

Adler, R. B., & Rodman, G. (1991). Understanding Human Communication. Toronto: Holt Rinehart and Winston.

Arini, A. T. (2012). Persepsi Risiko di Indonesia: Tinjauan Kualitatif Sistematik. *Buletin Psikologi, 20*(1–2), 66–81.

Aryani, F., Raden, A., & Ismarwati. (2017). Senam Hamil Berpengaruh terhadap Tingkat Kecemasan pada Primigravida Trisemester III di RSIA Sakina Idaman Sleman D.I. Yogyakarta. *Jurnal Ners dan Kebidanan Indonesia, 4*(3), 129–134, doi: 10.21927/jnki.2016.4(3).

Hermawati, I., Hartanti, & Lasmono, H. K. (1994). Hubungan Antara Kecemasan Pada Kehamilan Akhir Triwulan Ketiga Dengan Lama Persalinan Pada Ibu Yang Melahirkan Anak Pertama. *Anima, IX*(34), 63–68.

Kaplan, H. I., Sadock, B. J., & Grebb, J. A. (1994). *Sinopsis Psikiatri*. 1(7). alih bahasa: Wijaya Kusuma. Jakarta: Binarupa Aksara.

Kartono, K. (2007). *Psikologi Wanita (Jilid 2) Mengenal Wanita Sebagai Ibu dan Nenek*. Bandung: CV Mandiri Maju.

Lifshitz, R., Nimrod, G., & Bachner G. Yaacov. (2016). Measuring Risk Perception in Later Life: The Perceived Risk Scale. *Journal of the American Psychiatric Nurses Association, 22*(6), 469–474, doi: 10.1177/107839031665991.

Nevid, J. S., Rathus, S. A., & Greene B. (2005). Pengantar Psikologi Abnormal. Bandung: Erlangga.

Pargament, K. I., Koening, H. G., & Perez, L. M. (2000). The Many Methods of Religious Coping: Development and Initial Validation of the RCOPE. *Journal of clinical psychology, 58*(4), 519–543.

Pargament, K., Feuille, M., & Burdzy, D. (2011). The Brief RCOPE: Current Psychometric Status of a Short Measure of Religious Coping. *Religions, 2*(1) (Measures of Spirituality/Religiosity), 51–76.

Peak, H.-J., & Hove, T. (2017). Risk Perceptions and Risk Characteristics. *Oxford Research Encyclopedia of Communication*, 1–14.

Pieter, Z. H. & Lubis, B. (2013). Psikologi untuk Bidan Suatu Teori dan Penerapannya. Yogyakarta: Rapha Publishing.

Reza, I. F. (2015). *Mengatasi Kerentanan Stres Melalui Coping Religious*. Yogyakarta: PT. Kanisius.

Reza, I. F. (2016). Implementasi Coping Religious dalam Mengatasi Gangguan Fisik-Psikis-Sosial-Spiritual pada Pasien Gagal Ginjal Kronik. *Intizar, 22*(2), 243–280.

Schetter, D. Christine. (2011). Psychological Science on Pregnancy: Stress Processes, Biopsychosocial Models, and Emerging, Research Issues. *Annual Review Psychology, 62*, 531–558, doi: 10.1146/annurev.psych.031809.130727.

Sue, D., Sue, D. W., Sue, D., & Sue, S. (2010). *Understanding Abnormal Behavior Eighth Edition*. New York: Houghton Mifflin Company.

Yang benar, Rahman, A.A. (2016). *Metode Penelitian Psikologi*. Bandung: PT Remaja Rosadakarya.

Sri Maslihah[1], Irfan Fahmi[2], and Anastasia Wulandari[1]

The Role of Spirituality and Parental Support in Psychological Well-Being of Juvenile Offenders

Universitas Pendidikan Indonesia, Indonesia[1]
Universitas Islam Negeri Sunan Gunung Djati Bandung, Indonesia[2]

Abstract. This study aims to examine the role of spirituality and parental support in psychological well-being on juvenile offenders. Researchers used a quantitative approach by distributing a questionnaire to 105 juvenile offenders. Measurements of spirituality, parental support, and psychological well-being were used in the questionnaire. The data was then analyzed using a multiple regression. The results show that both spirituality and parental support had a simultaneous effect on the psychological well-being of juvenile offenders with a contribution value of 54.8%. This finding highlights the importance of parental support in the lives of juvenile offenders.

Keywords: Spirituality, parental support, psychological well-being, juvenile offenders

1 Introduction

The ideal hope of society is that children can grow and develop optimally so that they have a healthy, intelligent, cheerful, and independent physical and mental condition to be ready to carry out responsibilities according to their age. It is the duty of parents, society, and the state to support children so that, when the time comes, the children are ready to continue the leadership role from the previous generation. Child Protection Law No. 23 of 2002 / Law No.35 of 2014 concerning Substitutes states, "A child is someone who is not yet 18 years old, including children in the womb."

In the process of growth and development, there are a few children who have to deal with legal problems. While, at their age, they should be occupied with activities to develop themselves, these children undergo a series of legal process as adults involved in legal cases. Data from the Directorate General of Corrections shows that as of March 2018, there were 3,323 children aged 14–18 years old incarcerated at the Youth Correctional Center/Lembaga Pembinaan Khusus Anak (hereinafter abbreviated as LPKA) in Indonesia because they were involved in various criminal acts.

These incarcerated children (hereinafter referred to as juveniles) who live in LPKA (formerly known as Lapas Anak) and attend a training program for their committed criminal act are faced with an array of consequences, such as losing their physical freedom, control over life, family, goods and services, security, and heterosexual relationships, as well as lacking of stimulation and possibility of having psychological disorders (Cooke et al., 1990). These juveniles also face various problems not only from within LPKA, such as inadequate facilities and violence, either by other students or officers, but also from outside LPKA, such as family and community problems (Cooke et al., 1990).

The above phenomenon indicates that LPKA lacks adequate regulations, facilities, and infrastructure, as well as supportive environment. This condition affects the psychological well-being of the juveniles because after all they are required to adapt. The LPKA environment that keeps juveniles away from freedom and separated from their closest people, such as family and peers, leads them to be vulnerable to various psychological disorders, jeopardizing their psychological well-being. As stated by Laan and Eichelsheim (2013), violence or psychological pressure in the prison or correctional process is a stressor as well as a traumatic event that can affect the psychological well-being of the juveniles.

The need for mental health and well-being is more discussed among juveniles living/occupying LPKA-like institutions than those living outside of LPKA (Hagel, in Khan, 2010). This is due to the complex psychological problems that can arise as a result of separation from the outside world and the systems within the institution itself. Based on the results of the study, 18% of juveniles attending a training program at an LPKA-like institution experience depression, 10% experience anxiety disorders, and 5% experience psychotic symptoms. Moreover, half of them experience a conduct disorder. The same study also shows that eight out of 10 juveniles living in LPKA suffered from mental health problems based on a formal diagnosis (Christabesan, Fazel et al., in Khan, 2010).

Obstacles in fulfilling the needs for the juveniles to develop in relation to their presence in LPKA potentially will become stressors that causes psychological problems. Meanwhile, these juveniles have no options other than attending the training program. Considering that this research will use a positive psychological approach, researchers intend to explore how the juveniles interpret the situation in LPKA and urge them to explore positive meanings behind the unpleasant situation.

The concept of psychological well-being (hereinafter referred to as PWB) states that well-being is determined by the ability of an individual to function positively in his life (Ryff, 1995). The construct of PWB was adopted to represent the eudemonic tradition, with a focus on skill development and personal growth, both understood as key indicators of positive individual functioning (Diaz et al., 2006). Furthermore, the essence of eudaimonia is to strive towards excellence based on one's potential and unique characteristics. This understanding is used by Ryff to explain the psychological conception of well-being which is explicitly related to individual self-development and realization (Ryff & Singer, 2006).

According to Ryff (1995), psychological well-being is a term used to describe an individual's psychological health based on fulfilling the criteria for positive psychological function. Psychological well-being is a condition of a healthy individual characterized by the functioning of positive psychological aspects in the process of achieving self-actualization. Ryff's (1989) construct of psychological well-being aspects include self-acceptance, personal growth, purpose in life (purposive with life), environmental mastery, autonomy, and positive relationships with people.

Several researchers have shown that psychological well-being is not a stand-alone concept but is influenced by several factors. Schmutte and Ryff (1997) added that psychological well-being can be influenced by various aspects of an individual, namely gender, social class, and ethnic status. Ryff's research (1989; 1991; 1995; 1998) shows that age is one of the factors that influences psychological well-being. Some aspects of psychological well-being show an increase with increasing age, while other aspects show slight variations and a decrease with increasing age. In the aspect of environmental control, autonomy, self-acceptance, and positive relationships, it shows an increase with an increasingly mature age. Meanwhile, life goals and personal growth show a sharp decline in each period of adult life (Ryff in Snyder & Lopez, 2002).

Another study related to factors that influence psychological well-being was conducted by Mukolo and Wallston (2012). Their research on people living with HIV found that psychological well-being of people living with HIV was closely related to three personal coping resources, namely a sense of coherence, an optimistic outlook on life, and belief. This belief is often known as self-efficacy which is predicted to be able to provide positive changes in psychological well-being over time. Mukolo and Wallston's research strengthens previous studies (Ryff et al., 1989; 1995; 2006; Snyder & Lopez, 2002) that state that internal factors in the subject, especially belief, will have an impact on increasing psychological well-being of an individual.

Regarding internal factors in individuals, especially in the context of individuals in correctional institutions, Liwarti (2013) states that spiritual experience is one of the factors that increases and thought to be closely related to psychological well-being. This is reinforced by the findings of Allen et al. (2008) that state that having more daily spiritual experiences and not feeling abandoned by God increase positive emotions that create a positive effect on psychological well-being. According to Roof (in Frey, 2005), in psychology, the characteristics of spirituality are presented as a network of theoretical relationships in the area of well-being (psychological well-being/happiness).

According to Koening and Siegler (in Liwarti, 2013), spirituality is a source of coping that is usually performed by individuals who experience sadness, loneliness, and loss. When experiencing events that evoke feelings of sadness, fear, and loss, most people will remember God again. This will be an addition to their spiritual experiences. Spirituality in the lives of youth is crucial because the value of spirituality will be used as the basis of their lives to deal with conflicts in turbulent periods (Idrus, 2003).

Spirituality is not always synonymous with religion although one of the sources of spirituality can be found in religion. The word "spirituality" refers to the tendency of humans to seek meaning in life through self-transcendence or the need to connect to things bigger than the individual, as stated by Zinbauger, Pargament, and Scott (in Compton, 2005).

Myers and Williard (in Paloutzian & Park, 2013) define spirituality as the transcendent capacity and presence in life to find and construct meaning. Meanwhile, Pargament (in Snyder & Lopez, 2002) defines spirituality as a quest to be holy. There are two keywords in the definition, namely seeking and holy. The word "search" is identified as a process that involves seeking to find holiness and trying to hold on to the holiness that has been found. The word holy involves the concept of God and transcendent.

Burkhardt (1998) defines spirituality as a driving force, life principle, or essence that penetrates life and is expressed in (1) relationships with God; (2) relationships with oneself; (3) relationships with others; and (4) relationships with the environment. This definition of spirituality from Burkhadt is the concept of spirituality that researchers used in this study and becomes the basis for measuring instruments for spirituality.

Apart from spirituality, another factor related to psychological well-being is social support. It is an individual external factor that can affect psychological well-being. As found by Puspita (2013), perception of social support from family has a significant effect on the psychological well-being of the juveniles. Previously, several researchers indicated that social support, especially family support, is also an important source in the lives of the juveniles in LPKA (Born, et al., 1997; Carr & Vandiver, 2001; Feinstein, 2008).

Family support is crucial for adolescents. Research results consistently prove a positive relationship between family/parent support and the positive effects of stress. Demaray and Malacki (2002), for example, found that ethnically diverse adolescents who perceive to have a high level of parental support show higher levels of interpersonal adjustment as well as the absence of maladjustment. Windle (1992) also found that adolescents with less parental support involve more in delinquency. Family support is a crucial factor for youth resilience during their time in LPKA (Born, et al., 1997; Carr & Vandiver, 2001; Feinstein et al., 2008). In addition, social support as an external factor that come from the environment for the juveniles in LPKA is perceived as support from family, peers, and officers of special guidance institutions for children (Maslihah, 2017a).

Weiss (in Cutrona et al., 1994) divides social support into six parts based on the relationships with other individuals. This concept underlies social support measurement tools in this study. The six forms of social support include (1) guidance, namely social support in the form of advice and information from reliable sources; (2) reliable alliance, namely the knowledge that the individuals have that they can rely on real help when needed; (3) attachment, namely the expression of affection and love received by individuals to provide a sense of security; (4) reassurance of worth, namely in the form of recognition or appreciation of individual abilities and qualities; (5) social integration, in the form of shared interests and concerns as well as a sense of belonging in a group; and (6) opportunity to provide nurturance, in the form of individual feelings that they are needed by others.

Referring to the explanation above, the research problem in this study is as follows: "Do spirituality as an internal factor and social support from parents as an external factor have a simultaneous and significant effect on psychological well-being of the juveniles in LPKA?"

2 Method

This study aims to determine how spirituality and parental support influence the psychological well-being of the juveniles in LPKA. Researchers applied an explanatory research design to analyze the relationships between one variable and another or how a variable affects other variables (Neuman, 2007).

The method used in this research is a quantitative method, which is a method for testing certain theories by examining the relationship between variables. These variables are usually measured using research instruments to statistically analyzed numerical data (Creswell, 2009). Researchers then implemented a path analysis technique to analyze the data.

2.1 Sample

The sampling technique used in this study is non-probability sampling, in which not all members of the population have the same opportunity to become a sample unit. Subjects who were the sample units were the juveniles in LPKA Tangerang who had served a sentence for more than six months, assuming that they have undergone a period of adjustment to the LPKA environment. Meanwhile, the sampling technique used was accidental sampling, in which researchers took samples from members of the population with predetermined characteristics who were available at that time of sampling. From this technique, researchers took 105 juveniles as samples.

2.2 Measurement Tools

The variables used in this study are (a) independent variables, namely Spirituality and Parental Support (social support); and (b) dependent variable, namely psychological well-being.

The data collection technique was carried out through a measuring instrument in the form of a questionnaire, consisting of (1) Spirituality, compiled by Urie (2014) based on Burkhardt's concept of spirituality to measure the level of spirituality; (2) Parental Support, compiled by the researchers themselves based on Weiss's concept of social support to measure parental support; and (3) Psychological Well-being, compiled by Urie (2014 based on Ryff's concept of psychological well-being) to measure the psychological well-being.

Researchers then tested the reliability and validity of all measuring instruments of the research variables using the SPSS Statistics V21. For the selection of a feasible item, researchers tried out the number of items in all variables. After the tryout was carried out, item analysis was performed, and only items with a corrected item – total correlation value above 0.3 – were selected to represent the indicator. Through testing and selecting items that are feasible or discarding items that are not feasible (corrected item-total correlation <0.3), the final reliability value of the measuring instrument can be seen in Table 1.

Table 1. Reliability of Measuring Instruments

Variables	Cronbach's Alpha	Notes
Spirituality	0.916	Reliable
Parental Support	0.946	Reliable
Psychological Well-Being	0.932	Reliable

Data analysis was performed by applying the path analysis method using the SPSS Statistics V21. See table 2.

3 Results

The research hypothesis is as follows: "There is a simultaneous relationship between Spirituality and Parental Support in the Psychological Well-Being of the juveniles in LPKA," and the sub-hypothesis of this research are as follows:

(1) Spirituality affects the psychological well-being (PWB) of the juveniles in LPKA.
(2) Parental support affects the psychological well-being (PWB) of the juveniles in LPKA. The results of the calculation of path analysis using the SPSS Statistics V21 are as follows:

Table 2. Correlations

		Spirituality	Parental Support	PWB
Spirituality	Pearson Correlation	1	,345**	,560**
	Sig. (2-tailed)		,000	,000
	N	105	105	105
Parental Support	Pearson Correlation	,345**	1	,647**
	Sig. (2-tailed)	,000		,000
	N	105	105	105
PWB	Pearson Correlation	,560**	,647**	1
	Sig. (2-tailed)	,000	,000	
	N	105	105	105

**. Correlation is significant at the 0.01 level (2-tailed).

The results of the path analysis for the first hypothesis showed that the path coefficient of 0.382 obtained a significance value of 0.000 (See picture 1) with a sig.0.000 value. Since the value is smaller than the probability value 0.05 (0.00 <0.05), it means Ho is rejected, and Ha is accepted. This shows that the path analysis coefficient is significant, indicating that spirituality has an effect on psychological well-being. Thus, spirituality, as the transcendent capacity and presence in life to find and construct meaning, (Myers & Williard, in Paloutzian & Park, 2013) needs to be honed in the process of fostering juveniles in LPKA. As stated by Burkhardt (1998), spirituality is a force that moves or an essence that

Table 3. Coefficients

Model		Unstandardized Coefficients		Standardized Coefficients	T	Sig.
		B	Std. Error	Beta		
1	(Constant)	113,157	10,769		10,508	,000
	Spirituality	,537	,100	,382	5,381	,000
	Parental Support	,437	,060	,516	7,266	,000

a. Dependent Variable: PWB

Table 4. Model Summary

Model	R	R Square	Adjusted R Square	Std. Error of the Estimate	Change Statistics				
					R Square Change	F Change	df1	df2	Sig. F Change
1	,740[a]	,548	,539	13,228	,548	61,722	2	102	,000

a. Predictors: (Constant), Parental Support, Spirituality

b. Dependent Variable: PWB

Table 5. ANOVA

Model		Sum of Squares	Df	Mean Square	F	Sig.
1	Regression	21600,650	2	10800,325	61,722	,000[b]
	Residual	17848,340	102	174,984		
	Total	39448,990	104			

a. Dependent Variable: PWB

b. Predictors: (Constant), Parental Support, Spirituality

penetrates life and can be expressed in (1) relationships with God; (2) relationships with oneself; (3) relationships with others; and (4) relationships with the environment. The discovery of life's meaning, either through a relationship with God, with oneself, with other people, or with the environment, supports psychological well-being of the juveniles even though they have to live separately from their home environment.

The results of this study also support the statement that spiritual experiences are thought to be closely related to psychological well-being (Liwarti, 2013). This is reinforced by the findings of Allen, Philips, Roof, Cavanaugh, and Day (in Mandouj et al, 2013) that by having more spiritual experiences in life and not feeling abandoned by God increase positive emotions that leads to a positive effect on psychological well-being.

Furthermore, to test the second hypothesis, the results of the path analysis showed that the path coefficient of 0.516 obtained a significance value of 0.000 (Table 3). The sig.0,000 value means smaller than the probability value 0.05; therefore, Ho is rejected, and Ha is accepted. This shows that the path analysis coefficient is significant, indicating that parental support affects psychological well-being.

The findings of this study reinforce the results of research by Solichatun (2012) and Maslihah (2017) regarding the urgency of parental support for juveniles in LPKA. This is inseparable from the psychological development of juveniles in LPKA who are in their teenage years. The age of transition from childhood to adulthood shows that they are not yet independent adults. Juveniles in LPKA are children who still need guidance, attention, and affection from their parents or family. Therefore, social support from parents is needed in achieving the psychological well-being of the juveniles in LPKA.

Through the calculation of this path analysis (see figure 1), we obtained that the effect of spirituality on psychological well-being is 0.3822 = 0.146 or 14.6%, and the effect of parental support on psychological well-being is 0.5162 = 0.266 or 26.6%. Meanwhile, the simultaneous influence of spirituality and social support on psychological well-being is $R^2 = 0.548$ (54.8%). The rest of 0.452 (45.2%)

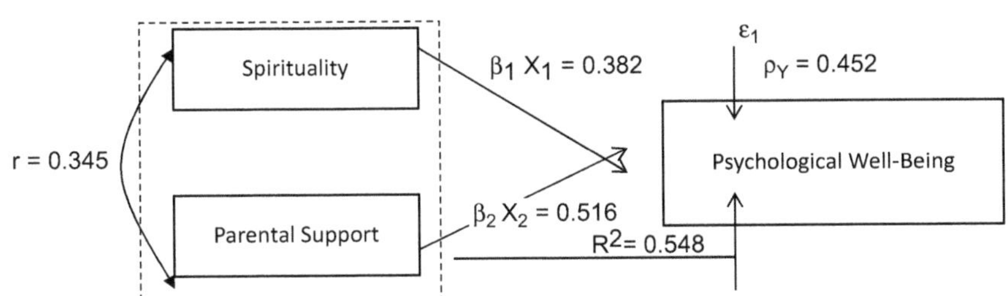

Figure 1. Path Analysis of the Correlation Between Spirituality, Parental Support, and Psychological Well-Being on Juvenile Offenders

is influenced by other factors that are not explained in this study. The simultaneous presence of spirituality and parental support as an internal and external factor for the psychological well-being of the juveniles in LPKA has a greater influence than the individual influence of each spirituality and parental support on psychological well-being.

The results of the path analysis indicate that there are other factors besides spirituality and parental support that can affect the psychological well-being of the juveniles in LPKA, both from internal and external. As Mirowsky and Ross (in Ryan & Deci 2006) state, there are various conditions that can affect a person's psychological well-being, including economic power, employment, education, children, one's childhood, and physical health.

Furthermore, Bhogle and Prakash (1995) explain that there are several factors that affect psychological well-being, namely: (1) Self-Control (the ability of a person to control all emotions and drives that arise within himself); (2) Self-Esteem (having a balanced self-esteem); (3) Positive Affectivity (positive feelings or emotions); (4) Tension Management (the ability to regulate tension that comes out of within, for example, anger or happiness, so that they do not appear excessively); (5) Positive Thinking (the ability to think positively when dealing with new events, situations, or individuals); and (6) Efficient Idea and Feeling (issuing ideas and feelings that are right and appropriate to the context and not excessive).

Based on the explanation above, it can be concluded that psychological well-being is influenced by internal factors originating from the individual and external factors originating from the environment. Spirituality is an internal factor, while social support from parents is an external factor affecting psychological well-being (Solichatun, 2012, Maslihah, 2017a).

Apart from parental support, peer support is also essential in the lives of the juveniles in LPKA (Born et al., 1997; Carr & Vandiver, 2001; Feinstein, 2008). Peer interaction and acceptance in LPKA remain a necessity for the juveniles in LPKA, as stated by Whitehead and Steptoe (2007). According to Whitehead and Steptoe (2007), building friendship in LPKA is an important aspect of adjustment in LPKA. Social support and acceptance of friends are also major predictors of the psychological well-being of the juveniles in LPKA.

In addition, Solichatun (2012) in his research on juveniles in LPKA Blitar also explains that social support for juveniles in LPKA is mostly obtained from peers and LPKA, in the form of emotional support of officers as well as instrumental support and information. LPKA officers interact daily with the juveniles and can be the first adults to ask about the condition of the juveniles when facing difficulties. This situation creates a stronger dependency of the juveniles on the officers considering that the officers can be present in all situations for the juveniles during their time in LPKA (Maslihah, 2017b). This reinforces the findings of Edwards (2008) that state that social support also comes from the prison environment, namely fellow inmates and prison officers who assist inmates in their process of adjustment.

4 Conclusion

The results obtained indicate that spirituality and parental support simultaneously influence psychological well-being. The contribution value given by spirituality and parental support to psychological well-being simultaneously is greater than the influence given by spirituality and parental support individually on psychological well-being. This means that the presence of these two variables is significantly necessary to achieve the psychological well-being of the juveniles in LPKA. However, the contribution value of spirituality and parental support to psychological well-being is only 54.8%. This shows that 45.2% of the psychological well-being of the juveniles in LPKA can be influenced by other factors, both from internal and external, aside from spirituality and parental support.

For further research, referring to the results of this study, it is suggested to explore other factors that influence psychological well-being, specifically the psychological well-being of the juveniles in LPKA. Practically, this research provides recommendations for LPKA and parents of the juveniles to create a conducive environment for the psychological well-being of the juveniles in LPKA.

5 Affiliations

1. Name: Sri Maslihah
Institution: Universitas Pendidikan Indonesia, Indonesia
Address: Jl. Dr. Setiabudi No.229 Bandung, Indonesia
E-mail: maslihah_psi@upi.edu

2. Name: Irfan Fahmi
Institution: UIN Sunan Gunung Djati Bandung
Address: Jl. A.H. Nasution No 105 Kota Bandung
E-mail: irfan.fahmi@uinsgd.ac.id

3. Name: Anastasia Wulandari
Institution: Universitas Pendidikan Indonesia, Indonesia
Address: Jl. Dr. Setiabudi No.229 Bandung, Indonesia
E-mail: diangem2_psi@upi.edu

6 References

Allen, R., Phillips, L., Roff, L., Cavanaugh, R., & Day, L. (2008) Religiousness/spirituality and mental health among older male inmates. *Gerontologist, 48*(5), 692–697.

Bhogle, S., & Prakash, I. J. (1995). Development of the Psychological Wellbeing (PWB) questionnaire. *Journal of Personality and Clinical Studies, 11*, 5–9.

Born, M., Chevalier, V., & Humblet, I. (1997). Resilience, desistance and delinquent career of adolescent offenders. *Journal of Adolescent, 20*, 679–694.

Burkhardt, M. A. (1989). Spirituality: An analysis of the concept. *Holistic Nursing Practice, 3*(3), 69–77.

Carr, M. B., & Vandiver, T. A. (2001). "Risk and protective factors among youth offenders." *Adolescence,* 36(143), 409–426.

Cooke, D. J., Baldwin, P. J., & dan Howison, J. (1990). *Psychology in prisons.* London: Routledge.

Compton, W. C. (2005). *Introduction to positive psychology*. USA: Wadsworth.

Cutrona, C. E., et al. (1994). Perceived parental social support and academic achievement: an attachment theory perspective. *Journal of Personality and Social Psychology, 66*(2), 369–378.

Demaray, M. K., & Malecki, C. K. (2002). Critical levels of perceived social support associated with student adjustment. *School Psychology Quarterly, 17*, 213–241.

Diaz, D., Rodriguez-Carvajal, R., Blanco, A., Moreno-Jimenez, B., Gallardo, I., & Valle, C. (2006). Spanish adaptation of the Psychological Well-Being Scales (PWBS). *Psicothema, 18*, 572–577.

Edward, W. T. (2008). *How do variations in social support resources of prisoners correlate with psychological distress*. Abstract of Dissertation. University of Kentucky (online). (Akses: 13/12/13).

Feinstein, L. B. (2008). *The social and personal benefits of learning: A summary of key research findings*. London: Centre for Research on the Wider Benefits of Learning, Institute of Education

Frey, B. B.,dkk. (2005). *University of Kansas Measuring a dimension of spirituality in personality*. New York: Guilford.

Idrus, Muhammad. (2003). *Kecerdasan Spiritual Mahasiswa Yogyakarta*. Yogyakarta: Universitas Islam Indonesia.

Khan, L. (2010). *Reaching out, reaching in: Promoting mental health & emotional wellbeing in secure setting*. Center of Mental Health.

Laan, A., & Eichelsheim, V. (2013) Juvenile adaptation to imprisonment: Feelings of safety, autonomy and well-being, and behavior in prison. *European Journal of Criminology* (online), *10*(4): 424–443.

Liwarti. (2013). *Hubungan Pengalaman Spiritual dengan Psychological well-being Penghuni Lembaga Pemasyarakatan*. Universitas MuhammadiyahMalang. Volume I (1), 77–88. Tersedia: ejournal.umm.ac.id. (Akses 13/11/2013).

Maslihah, S. (2017a). Faktor yang Mempengaruhi Kesejahteraan Subyektif Anak Didik Lembaga Pembinaan Khusus Anak. *Jurnal Psikologi Insight, 1*(1), 82–94.

Maslihah, S. (2017b). Pengaruh Strategi Koping dan Dukungan Petugas terhadap Kesejahteraan Psikologis Integratif Anak Didik Lembaga Pembinaan Khusus Anak. Disertasi. Universitas Padjadjaran (tidak diterbitkan).

Mukolo, A., & Wallston, K. A. (2012). The relationship between positive psychological attributes and psychological well-being in persons with HIV/AIDS. *Journal AIDS Behavior, 16*, 2374–2381.

Neuman, W. L. (2007). *Basics of social research: Quantitative and qualitative approaches* (2nd ed.). Boston: Allyn and Bacon.

Paloutzian, R. F., & Park, C. L. (2013). *Handbook of the psychology of religion and spirituality*. USA: Guilford Press:

Puspita, H. N. (2013). *Pengaruh Self Esteem dan Perceived Social Support Terhadap Psychological Well-Being Anak Didik LPKA Anak Pria Tangerang*. Ringkasan Skripsi: Universitas Islam Negeri Syarif Hidayatulloh (tidak diterbitkan).

Ryan, R. M., & dan Deci, E. L. (1989). "On happiness and human potentials: A review of research on Hedonic and Eudaimonic Well-Being". *Annual Reviews Psychology, 52*, 141–166.

Ryff, C. D., & dan Keyes, C. L. M. (1995). "The structure of psychological well-being revisited". *Journal of Personality and Social psychology, 69*, 719–727

Ryff, C. D., Singer, B., Love, G. D., & Essex, M. J. (1998). Resilience in adulthood and later life: Defining features and dynamic processes. In J. Lomranz (Ed.), *Handbook of aging and mental health: An integrative approach* (pp. 69–96). New York: Plenum Press.

Ryff, C. D., & Singer, B. (2006). "Psychological well-being and ill-being: Do they have distinct or mirrored biological correlates?". *Psychotherapy and Psychosomatics, 75*, 85–95.

Solichatun, Y. (2012). *Regulasi Emosi dan Dukungan Sosial sebagai Moderator Hubungan Stres dan Resiliensi pada Anak Didik di Lembaga Pemasyarakatan Anak.* Disertasi. Universitas Gajah Mada (Tidak Diterbitkan)

Snyder, C., & Lopez, S. (2002). Positive pychology. dalam *Handbook of positive psychology.* New York: Oxford University Press.

Urie, B. E. (2014). *Penyusunan Alat Ukur Spiritualitas dan Kesejahteraan Psikologis.* Artikel Clinical Psychology (tidak diterbitkan).

Undang-Undang Republik Indonesia nomor 34 tahun 2014 tentang Pengganti Undang-Undang Republik Indonesia no.23 tahun 2002 tentang Perlindungan Anak.

Windle, M. (1992). Temperament and social support in adolescence: Interrelations with depressive symtomps and delinquent behaviors. *Journal of Youth and Adolescence, 21*(1), 1–21.

Whitehead, D. L., & Steptoe, A. (2007). *Prison.* In Fink, G. (Ed.), *Encyclopedia of stress* (2nd ed., Vol. 3, pp. 217–221). e-book edition.

N. Kardinah, Elisa Kurniadewi, and Sari Gita Suryana

Wisdom and Knowledge of Single Mothers Who Have Special Needs Children

Universitas Islam Negeri Sunan Gunung Djati Bandung, Indonesia

Abstract. The purpose of the study is to find out the description of wisdom and knowledge of single mothers who have children with special needs. This research uses a qualitative method and employs a case study approach. The subjects consist of three single mothers who have children with special needs. The results of this study point out that single mothers of those special needs children who become clients at Rumah Terapi Aura have every character strength that forms the basis of the description of wisdom and knowledge, namely creativity, curiosity, open-mindedness, love of learning, and perspectives. All in all, the results of this study could be used by another similar institute which wishes to expand knowledge on parents who have special needs children.

Keywords: Strength of wisdom and knowledge, single mother, children with special needs

1 Introduction

It is commonly agreed that having a child gives a positive impact on a family, such as warmth, happiness when gathering with family members, and pride when the child has become a successful and useful person for others. In consequence, parents hold a responsibility to care and educate the child, because he/she is a mandate given by Allah SWT.

Teaching a child about faith and social life requires coordination of the child's body and soul. The soul includes the mental readiness of the child, while the body is all physical parts which constitute the body. The learning process will be more easily delivered and accepted if the child is born perfect. Unfortunately, there are children who are born mentally and physically imperfect.

Regarding physical limitations, parents may still understand how to take care of a special needs child from childhood to adulthood, but when it comes to mental limitations, sometimes parents are clueless about how to deal with it; even worse, some parents blame their children and label them to be "naughty." This signals parents' ignorance of the limitations possessed by their child.

In fact, parental support is needed by children with special needs in their development. However, in reality, not all parents in such a situation can accept and carry out their responsibilities and roles well towards children who have special needs. For instance, there are parents who choose to abandon their children and parents who choose to divorce from their spouse. Unluckily, the impact of a divorce will be felt by both the ex-husband and the ex-wife as they have to face drastic changes; note that after a divorce, both parents must still perform their respective responsibilities, which actually brings heavier load on them afterwards. The children will not be an exception to the impact.

Children who do not have a complete family can sometimes develop a low self-esteem, be excessively naughty, have underperforming learning achievements, and feel that they are lost. According to the results of several studies, nearly 60% of divorce cases in the United States and 75% in the UK involve the children. Even though there are provisions and laws regarding who is responsible for taking care of the child in the divorce case, the mother reaches 90% to take over the responsibility (Dagun, 2002, p. 113).

The above elucidation establishes the importance of this study. The role of children with special needs agency has a high impact on parents who have children with special needs. Thus, this study is hoped to give information about single parents, more specifically single mothers, who raise children with special needs.

2 Literature Review

Educating and raising children is not an easy task for a single parent, especially for women. They must educate their children while fulfilling their family's needs. In 2009, L'Namira explained the image of a tough woman who raised a baby alone without a companion to live with all her dynamics, while she also had to work to make a living to meet all the needs of her family members, hence functioning as both a mother and a father to her children. This is what the writers refer to as a single mother throughout this chapter.

As a parent, all women hope to have a healthy child, but in some cases, God gives them children with deficiencies. Children with deficiencies, both physically and mentally, are called children with special needs. These children have different needs from those of other children in general in living their life.

Wisdom is the basis formation of acceptance to the condition of children with special needs in a family. Meanwhile, knowledge about children is the basis on which a single mother can take care of her child properly. By knowing what kind of wisdom and knowledge about children with special needs is necessary, there will be real data about how likely it is that the child can develop in his/her family environment because going into a therapy alone will not have a significant impact on the development of the child.

High level of wisdom and knowledge will be good evaluation materials for agencies that conduct several case countermeasures, such as in the case of children with special needs and single mothers who have children with special needs, and for reducing the number of neglected children with special needs.

The wisdom and knowledge possessed by parents of children with special needs in psychological terms is referred to as Wisdom and Knowledge or, in the theory of Character Strength (Peterson Seligman, 2004), Virtue of Wisdom and Knowledge. Peterson and Seligman (2004) explain that Virtue of Wisdom and Knowledge is the use of information obtained to provide positive treatments and assistance to achieve a better life.

Wisdom and knowledge play a significant role in increasing resilience. This was studied by Yuliasi, Akmal (2017) on the role of wisdom and knowledge in students who experience academic stress. The results of this study show that virtue curiosity, perspectives, and creativity play a significant role in resilience.

In a study conducted by Lestari (2014), counseling guidance through bibliotherapy techniques can improve some aspects of students' wisdom and knowledge (Wisdom and Knowledge) character. Guidance and counseling through effective bibliotherapy techniques can also improve aspects of curiosity, open-mindedness (open thinking), and perspectives.

3 Method

This study is a qualitative research which uses a case study model. This method was used to find and explain the description of wisdom and knowledge on single mothers who have children with special needs at the Rumah Terapi Aura.

3.1 Sample

The subjects of this study were single mothers who have children with special needs. The subjects in this study were three individuals (RA, SA, and IR). They were single mothers aged over 30 years old who took care of themselves and lived with their children (aged between 5 to 12 years old). They became clients at Rumah Terapi Aura at least for three months and always participated in the listening of every evaluation given by the foundation.

3.2 Measurement Tools

The data collection techniques used in this study are interview and observation techniques which were conducted within three months. The data analysis was done by reflecting data obtained by using imaginative variation or structural description, looking for possible meanings and, through divergent perspectives, considering the framework for referencing symptoms (phenomenon), as well as constructing how these symptoms are experienced. After all the data had been processed, the researchers then constructed all the explanations about the meaning and essence of their experience. Data validity in qualitative research usually uses triangulation. Triangulation is a technique of checking the validity of data by using something else outside the data for the purpose of checking data or as a comparison to that data.

4 Results

To find out the description of wisdom and knowledge, the researchers base it on the theoretical analysis of Peterson and Seligman (2004). Peterson and Seligman (2004) explain that each person must have strength that is deeper than the strength of others; at least, every human has one strength of character which is the main force that will outgrow the strength of other characters.

Strength of wisdom and knowledge has several indicators, one of which is the strength of character. The strength of character in question includes the strength of creativity, strength of curiosity, strength of open-mindedness, strength of love of learning, and strength of perspectives.

The strength of creativity of the subjects is illustrated in their behavior when solving problems, including by being productive and able to establish social relations with their environment.

The strength of curiosity of the subjects is illustrated from the way they open themselves to the outside world, find out what they need, always look for experiences, and refrain from having specific expectations from their curiosity.

The subjects' strength of open-mindedness is seen from the fact that they can look for evidence or facts to strengthen their assumptions and can receive input from their environment. These two points can be seen from the extent to which they seek to find facts to strengthen their arguments so that new arguments can be accepted.

The subjects' strength of love of learning can be seen from how they can accept new knowledge and use that knowledge to provide new experiences and from the notion that there is a hope or purpose from the application of the knowledge obtained.

The last character strength that describes wisdom and knowledge is the strength of perspectives. The subjects' strength of perspectives can be illustrated in their broad view of things or problems; by viewing a problem to have a broad

Table 1. Result of This Study

Wisdom and Knowledge			
1. Creativity			
Problem solving	- Bring the child to workplace	- Entrust the child to neighbors	- Entrust the child to his/her sibling
Get income	- Work as a cook	- Work odd jobs	- Get pension fund and help from sibling
Social relation	- Be close to her sister and mother	- Be active in forums, close to family members	- Be active in forums, close to sibling
2. Curiosity			
Self-openness	- Be open to trust people	- Talk to and ask for help from family	- Always tell other people about her child's condition
Finding out what they need	- Search information on the Internet and ask other people	- Ask other people	- Ask other people
Looking for experience	- Look for experience to nurture her child	- Look for experience to teach her child	- Look for experience to teach her child
Not expecting anything from curiosity	- Only want to know about development of her child	- Only want to know the extent of her child's ability	- Only want to know the extent of her child's ability
3. Open-mindedness			
Proving the explanation	- Work so as to not bother other family members	- Ignore or frighten her child for being naughty	- Listen to mellow music and hug her child to comfort him/her
Accepting feedback	- Accept feedback but will process it after	- Accept feedback because it's a must	- Accept feedback and adjust it with her child's situation
4. Love of learning			
Accepting new knowledge	- Receive it from the Internet and Rumah Terapi Aura	- Receive it from seminars and social community	- Receive it from seminars and social community

(*continued*)

. Continued

Wisdom and Knowledge			
Accepting new experience	- Apply experience little by little	- Apply experience gradually and systematically	- Apply experience from outside into the house
Not expecting anything from it	- Only want her child to get better	- Only want her child to be independent	- Only want her child to be independent
5. Perspectives			
Having a broad perspective	- Think that special needs children only need more attention	- Think that special needs children will bring sustenance	- Think that children are also part of the community that must be accepted
Viewing a problem as having a broad meaning	- Think that a single mother faces financial difficulties but is more independent	- Think that a single mother is a trustworthy person for being able to pass life trials	- Think that a single mother has more insights about her children
Having positive values about herself and others	- Assume that her child gives more attention to others	- Assume that her child is more disciplined	- Assume that her child pays more attention to cleaning-up activities

meaning, they will be able to have a positive assessment of themselves and the others.

5 Conclusion

Based on the analysis conducted on the interviews and observations on the three subjects studied, Wisdom and Knowledge in single mothers who have children with special needs can be illustrated from the five strengths of the underlying character.

The first one is the strength of creativity. The strength of creativity of the single mothers has similarities. When they have dependents who need their support and at the same time they have to take care of their children with special needs, they prefer to invite their children to participate in their activities so that these two needs can still be fulfilled.

In dealing with problems caused by their children, the three subjects still use the same parenting style as other parents, but they are more responsive to the problems that occur and do not require their children to catch up.

Based on those explanations, it can be seen that single mothers of children with special needs have high strength of creativity, which can be seen from their ability to solve big problems, in terms of both financial and parenting duties towards their children.

The second strength of character is the strength of curiosity. The strength of curiosity of all the three subjects is also quite high because even though every parent has a different personality but basically all of them need a lot of information and always find this information by using various methods that are tailored to their personality, either by asking other people or based on personal experience.

The third strength of character is the strength of open-mindedness. The strength of open-mindedness of the single mothers studied also seems high because in addition to receiving input from their environment that will build and change their arguments, they also try to find evidence or facts to strengthen their arguments so that the input they receive can be processed and received correctly or partially.

The fourth character strength is the strength of love of learning. The strength of love of learning that is demonstrated by the subjects is also quite high because they know how the knowledge they have received and processed is used or applied to the core of the problem, especially regarding their child, and they also know the function, purpose, and use of the knowledge.

The fifth character strength is the strength of perspectives. The single mothers' strength of perspectives is also quite high because none of them finally considers children with special needs or their status as a single mother to be a problem. Instead, they always look at the problem from different perspectives, so they can still see the positive side of the problem.

Based on the above five character strengths, the researchers conclude that single mothers who have children with special needs at Rumah Terapi Aura have a high level of Wisdom and Knowledge. This is based on the five character strengths that are shown high even from subjects with different personalities.

The subjects have creativity in solving household problems, and they also have high curiosity so that they can understand what is needed. Moreover, because of their open-mindedness, they can receive new knowledge or facts to strengthen the assumptions they receive.

When the knowledge is received by them and creates new experiences that can be accepted, it changes their perspectives on the problem at hand and they can see the problem from the other side that has a positive value.

The results of this study can be used to describe that single mothers who have children with special needs have high values in their wisdom and knowledge. Agencies concerned about children with special needs could use the results of this study as materials to perform therapies on parents using their character strengths, such as basic materials for trainings, workshops, and knowledge transfer to educate parents, especially single mothers, on how to develop the way they nurture their children.

6 Affiliations

1. Name: N. Kardinah
Institution: Universitas Islam Negeri Sunan Gunung Djati Bandung
Address: Bandung City View 2 E-31 West Java
E-mail: n.kardinah@uinsgd.ac.id

2. Name: Elisa Kurniadewi
Institution: Universitas Islam Negeri Sunan Gunung Djati Bandung
Address: Cibiru Hilir cc6-24 Bandung West Java
E-mail: elisa.kurniadewi@uinsgd.ac.id

3. Name: Sari Gita Suryana
Institution: Universitas Islam Negeri Sunan Gunung Djati Bandung
Address: Solok, Sumatera Barat
E-mail: sari.suryana165@gmail.com

7 References

Andiani, Fauziah. (2016). Hubungan Antara Adversity Intelligence Dengan Keterbukaan Diri Pada Ibu Yang Memiliki Anak Autisme Di Kota Surakarta. *Jurnal Empati.* Vol. 5, No. 4.

Andrawina. (2017). Pengasuhan Keluarga Single Parent Terhadap Anak Berkebutuhan Khusus. *Jurnal Ilmiah Mahasiswa Universitas Airlangga.*

Badan Pusat Statistik. (2015). *Nikah, Talak, Cerai, Rujuk.*

Dagun, M. S. (2002). *Psikologi Keluarga.* Jakarta: Rineka Cipta.

Dariyo, A. (2003). *Psikologi Perkembangan Dewasa Muda.* Jakarta: Gramedia Widiasarana.

Desiningrum. (2016). *Psikologi Anak Berkebutuhan Khusus.* Yogyakarta: Psikosain.

Dwiyani. (2009). *Jika Aku Harus Mengasuh Anakku Seorang Diri.* Jakarta: Elex Media Komputindo.

Efendi, F., & Makhfudli. (2009). *Keperawatan Kesehatan Komunitas Teori & Praktek Dalam Keperawatan.* Jakarta: Salemba Medika.

Faqih, R. (2001). *Bimbingan Dan Konseling Dalam Islam.* Jogjakarta: UII Press.

Faradina, N. (2016). Penerimaan Diri Pada Orang Tua Yang Memiliki Anak Berkebutuhan Khusus. *Jurnal Psikologi.* ISSN: 2477–2674.

Gunarsa. (2008). *Psikologi Praktis: Anak Remaja dan keluarga.* Jakarta: BPK Gunung Mulia.

Hamidi. (2004). *Metode Penelitian Kualitatif Aplikasi Praktis Pembuatan Proposal dan Laporan Penelitian.* Malang: UMM Press.

Haryanto, Joko. (2012). *Transformasi dari Tulang Rusuk Menjadi Tulang Punggung.* Yogyakarta: Arti Bumi Intaran.

Hurlock, E. B. (1978). *Perkembangan Anak.* Jakarta: Erlangga. Terjemahan tahun 2004.

Ismatullah. (2015). Konsep Sakinah, Mawaddah, dan Rahmah Dalam Al-Qur'an. *Jurnal Pemikiran Hukum Islam Mazahib*, Vol. XIV, No. 1.

Kementerian Pemberdayaan Perempuan dan Perlindungan Anak Republik Indonesia. (2013). *Panduan Penanganan Anak Berkebutuhan Khusus bagi Pendampin (Orang Tua, Keluarga, dan Masyarakat.* Jakarta.

Kementerian Pendidikan dan Budaya. (2017). *Sekolah Inklusi dan Pembangunan SLB Dukung Pendidikan Inklusi.* Diunduh pada tanggal 1 januari 2018 dari https://www.kemdikbud.go.id/main/blog/2017/02/sekolah-inklusi-dan-pembangunan-slb-dukung-pendidikan-inklusi.

Kusumastuti, A. N. (2014). Stres Ibu Tunggal yang memiliki anak Autis. *Jurnal Psikologi.* Vol. 2, No. 7.

L'Namira, S. (2009). *La Tahzan for single mother.* Jakarta: Lingkar Pena Kreativa.

Laylliyah, Z. (2013). Perjuangan Hidup Single Parent. *Jurnal Sosiologi Islam.* Vol. 3, No. 1.

Lestari, S. (2014). *Psikologi Keluarga (Penanaman Nilai dan Penanganan Konflik dalam keluarga).* Jakarta: kharisma Putra Utama.

Mufidah, C. (2008). *Psikologi Keluarga Islam*. Malang: UIN Malang Press.

Muhammad, S. (2016). Fenomena Cerai Gugat di Kabupaten Kuningan. Vol. 9, No. 4.

Nurhadi. (2012). *Pendidikan Kedewasaan dalam Perspektif Islam.* Yogyakarta: Budi Utama.

Olivia, S. (2015). *Deteksi Dini Psikologi Balita hingga Manula.* Jakarta: Elex Media Komputindo.

Peterson dan Seligman. (2004). *Character strengths and virtues: A handbook and classification*. Oxford University Press.

Poerwandari, E. K. (2005). *Pendekatan Kualitatif Untuk Penelitian Perilaku Manusia (Edisi Ketiga).* Depok: LPSP3 Fakultas Psikologi Universitas Indonesia.

Raco. (2013). *Metode Penelitian Kualitatif Jenis Karakter dan Keunggulan.* Jakarta: Gasindo.

Rahim, A., Hussin, S., & Hassan, H. (2006). *Krisis & Konflik Institusi Keluarga.* Kuala Lumpur: Maziza SDN BHN.

Rasyid, H., & Hadi, S. (2016). *Panduan Muslim Sehari-Hari Dari Lahir Sampai Mati*. Jakarta: Wahyu Qolbu.

Reza. (2012). *Perilaku Konsumtif Pada Pria Metroseksual, Jurnal Ilmiah Mahasiswa Universitas Pendidikan Indonesia*, Bandung.

Setyowati, Uyun. (2014). *Kebermaknaan Hidup pada janda.* Jurnal Ilmiah Mahasiswa. Jurnal Psikologi Universitas Muhammadiyah. Surakarta.

Sugiyono. (2006). *Metode Penelitian Kuantitatif, Kualitatif, dan R&D.* Bandung: Alfabeta.

Sugiyono. (2013). *Metode Penelitian Pendidikan Pendekatan Kuantitatif, Kualitatif, dan R&D.* Bandung: Alfabeta.

Surbakti, E. B. (2008). *Sudah Siapkah Menikah?.* Jakarta: Elex Media Koputindo.

Undang-Undang Republik Indonesia Nomor 1 tahun 1974 Tentang Perkawinan.

Yin, R. K. (1996). *Studi Kasus Desain & Metode.* Jakarta: Raja Grafindo Persada.

Yin, K. (2011). *Qualitative research from start to finish*. Penerbit: The Guilford Press New York.

Yuliasih, Akmal. (2017). *Peran Wisdom Dan Knowledge Terhadap Resiliensi Pada Mahasiswa Yang Mengalami Stres Akademik.* Vol. 9, No. 2.

Yusuf. (2014). Dampak Perceraian Orang Tua Terhadap Anak. *Jurnal Al-Bayan.* Vol. 20, No. 29.

Zarina Akbar and Alyaa Pratiwi

Optimism and Family Resilience in Mothers of Children with Cerebral Palsy

Universitas Negeri Jakarta, Indonesia

Abstract. This study aims to determine the effect of optimism on family resilience in mothers who have children with cerebral palsy at the Disabled Children Development Foundation (YPAC) Jakarta. This study was conducted using a quantitative approach on 30 mothers who have children with cerebral palsy at YPAC Jakarta. Family resilience was measured using the Walsh Family Resilience Questionnaire, while Optimism was measured using instruments constructed by the researcher based on Seligman's theory of optimism. The statistical analysis used for testing the hypothesis is one predictor regression. The result calls for the need to explore more about family resilience in families with cerebral palsy.

Keywords: Family resilience, optimism, cerebral palsy

1 Introduction

In a family, having children with disabilities might have a great effect on all family members, including parents, siblings, and other family members (Reichman, Corman, & Noonan, 2008). One of the physical disabilities children may cope with is cerebral palsy, which is a disorder in controlling the movement function (Venty, Wibhawa, & Taftazani, 2015). According to Hinchcliffe (2007), the term "cerebral" refers to the brain, while "palsy" refers to weakness or paralysis. Cerebral palsy is, thus, a movement disorder caused by damage in the brain section (Hinchcliffe, 2007).

Parents of children with cerebral palsy experience an increase in stress levels compared to the general population of parents (Damgård, Sørensen, Vestrheim, Lerdal, Skranes, & Rohde, 2016). The pressure experienced by parents of children with cerebral palsy ranges from financial problems and health issues to the massive amount of time they spend to take care of their children instead of doing other activities (Wippermann, 2013). Parents who have children with cerebral palsy experience a greater personal burden and higher stress level, especially during the children's infancy, and this is generally experienced by mothers compared to fathers (Damgård et al., 2016).

Children with cerebral palsy in the severe category will need a lot of assistance in their daily activities, such as eating, bathing, and dressing. Taking care of these children also requires a significant amount of money, such as visits to doctor or other professionals, purchases of special equipment, and other additional necessities for the children (Bajraszewski, Carne, Kennedy, Lanigan, Ong, Randall, Reddthough, & Touzel, 2008). One of the integrated service centers for children with cerebral palsy is the Disabled Children Development Foundation (YPAC) Jakarta. Services for children with cerebral palsy at YPAC Jakarta are carried out in a one-stop service system that aims to facilitate parents in catering to the needs of their children by obtaining comprehensive and integrated services within the same institution.

A mother is considered as the main, important, and irreplaceable caregiver for her children and might be blamed for any problems occurring in the family (Walsh, 2006). Mother is the person most affected by the condition of her children; mother is considered as the main caregiver for the children. As a result, the mother often feels stressed and experiences psychological problems (depression, anxiety), physical problems (headache, high blood pressure), and feels greater pressure in carrying out her role as a mother and a wife (Azar & Badr, 2006).

Resilience could be interpreted as the capacity to rise from feeling difficulties and become stronger after going through a period of crisis and challenging events (Walsh, 2006). The term "family resilience" refers to processes in the family as a functional unit in overcoming and adapting to problems (Walsh, 2006). Resilient families are able to respond to the pressure or problems dealt with in a unique way, depending on the context of the problem itself, since the family might be resilient to certain problems but not resilient when facing other problems (Oh & Chang, 2014). Optimism is considered as an important key to resilience, which emphasizes strength, perseverance, courage, and acceptance (Walsh, 2006).

Many previous studies emphasize on the importance of family relationships in the development of optimism (Zanon et al., 2014). Optimistic parents tend to be better at taking care of their children more effectively since the optimists have a tendency to look at the bright side when facing an event (Labbé, Lopez, Murphy, & O'Brien, 2002). Therefore, the researcher was interested in conducting research on the effect of optimism on family resilience in mothers who have children with cerebral palsy at YPAC Jakarta. The result of this study is expected to bring a new perspective in understanding the form of resilience in families that have children with certain limitations.

2 Literature Review

2.1 Family Resilience

Family resilience refers to processes in the family as a functional unit in overcoming and adapting to problems (Walsh, 2006). Resilient families are able to respond to the pressure or problems in a unique way, depending on the context of the problem itself, because the family may be resilient to certain problems but not resilient when dealing with other problems (Oh & Chang, 2014). Walsh (2006) suggests three main dimensions in family resilience, namely belief systems, organizational patterns, and the communication process.

2.2 Optimism

Optimism is considered as an important key to resilience, which emphasizes strength, perseverance, courage, and acceptance (Walsh, 2006). Seligman (1995) reveals that there are three main dimensions of optimism, which he built based on the assumption that an individual's style of explaining the bad events which occur in his/her life (explanatory style) can determine whether the individual is an optimistic or perceptive person. The three dimensions are permanence, pervasiveness, and personalization.

3 Research Methodology

This study took a quantitative approach. The population being examined in this study were mothers who have children with cerebral palsy at the Disabled Children Development Foundation (YPAC) Jakarta. The sampling technique used in this study was a non-probability sampling. The researcher took a sample of 30 respondents who had certain characteristics in accordance with the research objectives. The following are the sample characteristics: mothers who were still in a marital status, who had a child with cerebral palsy aged 7–10 years old, and whose children were attending school or conducting a therapy at YPAC Jakarta.

There were two instruments used in this study, namely instruments to measure variables of family resilience and optimism. The instrument used to measure family resilience variables was the Walsh Family Resilience Questionnaire created by Walsh in 2012, which is based on three aspects of family resilience: (1) belief systems; (2) organizational patterns; and (3) communication process.

The instrument used to measure optimism variables was the construct that resulted from a measuring instrument of optimism carried out by the researcher based on Seligman's theory of optimism. Seligman divides optimism into three dimensions: (1) permanence (style of explaining events based on time); (2) pervasiveness (events based on scope); and (3) personalization (events based on the source of events).

4 Results and Discussion

The respondents who participated in this study totaled at 30 people. Based on the calculation, it is known that the research on family resilience level is at a low level with 17 respondents or equal to 56.7%. It is known that the research on optimism level is at a low level with 20 respondents or 66.7%.

This study used a hypothesis test regression analysis of one predictor using the *SPSS program version 16.0. The data analysis techniques were assisted by Winstep software* to find pure scores, then assisted by SPSS version 16.0 for regression analysis calculations.

Based on the statistical analysis, it was calculated that the constant variable family resilience is 1.11, while the regression coefficient of the optimism variable is 0.79. The significance test analyzed used ANOVA calculations, as seen in Table 1:

Table 1. Total Significance Test of ANOVA

Variable	**F**	***p* (sig)**
Optimism	3.73	0.064
Family Resilience		

Based on the result of the regression analysis from the SPSS support version 16.0, it was calculated that the F is 3.73 with the value $p > 0.05$ (not significant). Thus, it can be concluded that there is no significant effect between optimism and family resilience on mothers who have children with cerebral palsy at YPAC Jakarta.

Based on the hypothesis test obtained from the regression analysis test, it was stated that the hypothesis in this study was rejected, meaning that there is no significant influence between optimism and family resilience on mothers who have children with cerebral palsy.

In the previous study, it was explained that optimism had a significant relationship with family resilience in the context of poor colleges which received tuition fee accommodations for students (Nasa, 2012). However, in this study, which included mothers who have children with cerebral palsy at YPAC Jakarta as the research respondents, it is known that optimism does not have a significant effect on family resilience. The researcher assumed that there are other important factors that form a family resilience.

Family resilience is not formed because of the single contribution of the internal views of one family member. In a study on family resilience in palliative caregivers in Canada, it was found that family resilience was not only influenced by individual variables but also by the broader socio-environmental context, such as access to the social world, education, employment status, housing status, geographical location of residence, and life stages (Giesbrecht, Wolse, Crooks, & Stajduhar, 2015). According to Chang, Neo, and Fung (2015), there are several factors that form resilience in a family: (1) process factors, which include effective communication, altruistic sacrifice for family, love and care between each other; (2) structural factors, including strong leadership, unity, and interdependence on each other; (3) collective emotional management, for instance, normalizing moods, creating a lighter mood, and controlling negative feelings; and (4) making up meaning through a shared belief system, such as religion and worldview.

In another study conducted by Bayat (2007) regarding family resilience in families with autistic children, it was found that connectivity was the end result of families who were able to work well together. Families shall have two other qualities to strengthen connectivity, namely to be flexible and to communicate well to each other. Both of these qualities are needed since family members shall be flexible enough to accept changes in the roles and responsibilities needed as a result of the diagnosis on their children and to communicate to each other to successfully meet the new demands of the family. This indicates that family resilience is formed by the roles of fellow family members as a whole.

A study by Whittingham, Wee, Sanders, and Boyd (2011) found that parents of children with cerebral palsy faced very challenging conditions. Nevertheless, parents were also keen to promote communication, independence, and socialisation in their child. In addition, parents discussed the challenges of parenting under time pressure, with additional parenting tasks, under public scrutiny, and with grief. These may be effectively targeted as needs for a parenting intervention. In this condition, family resilience is very important to face those obstacles.

Family is a social institution and is one of the primary functions of society that is shaped by common agreements of males and females. Similar to other institutions, this social institution also has some duties like giving birth to a child, taking care of the child, teaching social behavior, giving education, and so forth. Therefore, the family is teaching and looking after the children, developing good communication between family members, and helping their children to perform independently. Even if a child is intellectually challenged, he/she is still one of the family members. When a family has a child with an intellectual disability, all family members will be impacted, including the siblings. In such a condition, all family members will likely face troubles and focus on the different abilities of the children. Parents may blame themselves or blame each other for the disability, start arguing, and sometimes end up having separation, divorce, psychological, and social problems (Kumar & Deepalatha, 2019).

The result of this research indicates that the level of optimism in mothers who have children with cerebral palsy at YPAC Jakarta is in the low category with a percentage of the population of 66.7%. According to the perspective of Flaskas (2007), it is important to understand family resilience neither as a lack of despair nor as a balance between hope and despair that can be mediated by all family members. A family member might remain optimistic and hopeful forever, thus balancing the despair of other family members. The processes in growing resilience might depend on the way the family maintains that balance (Power et al., 2016). Family resilience becomes a very important aspect. It shows that the more a family faces difficulties, the more the family learns. Family resilience changes the difficult situation into positive results, and this sometimes keeps them away from psychosocial problems.

Perlesz (1999, in Power, et al., 2016) states that family resilience allows for the ability to find meaning, acknowledge strength, survive, and coexist with negative feelings, such as experiencing pain, sadness, and anxiety related to the future and discomfort felt by the individuals in the family. Along with this opinion, the researcher then assumes that the insignificant effect of optimism on family resilience in this study is due to the disability of optimism to stand alone to form family resilience in mothers who have children with cerebral palsy, so attention should be paid to the finding of other variables that may accompany optimism to form a positive influence on family resilience. Some possible variables include uncertainty, social support, family assessment, coping skills, and problem solving (Shroff, 2014).

5 Conslusion

Based on the result of this study, there is no effect of optimism on family resilience in mothers who have children with cerebral palsy at YPAC Jakarta. The result of this study also shows that the level of optimism and family resilience in mothers who have children with cerebral palsy at YPAC Jakarta were, respectively, in the low category.

Based on the conclusions of this study, the researcher offers several suggestions. This research is expected to provide an overview for further research to consider qualitative research techniques in order to reveal more aspects in the formation of family resilience in families dealing with certain difficulties and to collect data in a wider scope, instead of limiting this to only one certain institution, to get broader views related to the psychological condition of mothers who have children with cerebral palsy.

6 Affiliations

Name:	Zarina Akbar
Institution:	Universitas Negeri Jakarta, Indonesia
Address:	Jl. Rawamangun Muka Raya, Rawamangun, Jakarta Timur
E-mail:	zarina_akbar@unj.ac.id

Name 2:	Alyaa Pratiwi
Surname:	
Institution:	Universitas Negeri, Jakarta
Address:	Jl. Rawamangun Muka Raya, Rawamangun, Jakarta Timur
Email:	alyaapratiwi1311@gmail.com

7 References

Azar, M., & Badr, L. K. (2006). The adaptation of mothers of children with intellectual disability in lebanon. *Journal of Transcultural Nursing, 17*(4), 375–380. doi: 10.1177/1043659606291550.

Bayat, M. (2007). Evidence of resilience in families of children with autism. *Journal of Intellectual Disability Research, 51*(9), 702–714. doi: 10.1111/j.1365-2788.2007.00960.x.

Benzies, K., & Mychasiuk, R. (2009). Fostering family resiliency: A review of the key protective factors. *Child and Family Social Work, 14*(1), 103–114. doi: 10.1111/j.1365-2206.2008.00586.x.

Chang, W. C., Neo, A. H. C., & Fung, D. (2015). In search of family resilience. *Psychology, 6*(13), 1594–1607. doi: 10.4236/psych.2015.613157.

Cheshire, A., Barlow, J., & Powell, L. (2010). Coping using positive reinterpretation in parents of children with cerebral palsy. *Journal of Health Psychology, 15*(6), 801–810. doi: 10.1177/1359105310369993.

Lerdal, B., Skranes, J., & Rohde, G. (2016). Optimism and sense of coherence in mothers and fathers of children with cerebral palsy participating in an intensified habilitation programme. *Scandinavian Journal of Disability Research, 18*(3), 245–255. doi: 10.1080/15017419.2015.1064025.

Frain, M. P., Berven, N. L., Chan, F., & Tschopp, M. K. (2008). Family resiliency, uncertainty, optimism, and the quality of life of individuals with

Giesbrecht, M., Wolse, F., Stajduhar, K., & Crooks, A. A. (2015). Identifying socio-environmental factors that facilitate resilience among Canadian palliative family caregivers. A qualitative case study. *Palliative & Supportive Care, 13*, 555–565. doi: 10.1017/S1478951513001028.

Kumar, K., & Deepalatha. (2019). Resilience and vulnerability in parents of child with intellectual disability (ID). *International Journal of Health Sciences and Research, 9*(5), 322-331.

Labbé, E. E., Lopez, I., Murphy, L., & O'Brien, C. (2002). Optimism and psychosocial functioning in caring for children with Battens and other neurological diseases. *Psychological Reports, 90*(3 Pt 2), 1129–35. doi: 10.2466/pr0.2002.90.3c.1129.

Oh, S., & Chang, S. J. (2014). Concept analysis: Family resilience. *Open Journal of Nursing,4*(4), 980–990. doi: 10.4236/ojn.2014.413105.

Power, J., Goodyear, M., Maybery, D., Reupert, A., O'Hanlon, B., Cuff, R., & Perlesz, A. (2016). Family resilience in families where a parent has a mental illness. *Journal of Social Work, 16*(1), 66–82. doi: 10.1177/1468017314568081.

Reichman, N. E., Corman, H., & Noonan, K. (2008). Impact of child disability on the family. *Maternal and Child Health Journal, 12*(6), 679–683. doi: 10.1007/s10995-007-0307-z.

Udin, R., & Suriyoko. (2014). Effect of automotive performance learning work practices and performance industry of interest in entrepreneurship. *Jurnal Taman Vokasi, 2*(1), 206–217.

Walsh, F. (2006). *Strengthening family resilience*. New York: The Guilford Press.

Warter, E. H. (2009). Promoting resiliency in families of individuals diagnosed with an autism spectrum disorder: The relationship between parental beliefs and family adaptation. Boston College. *Thesis.*

Whittingham, K., Wee, D., Sanders, M., & Boyd, R. (2011). Responding to the challenges of parenting a child with cerebral palsy: a focus group. *Disability and Rehabilitation, 33*, 1557–1567. DOI: 10.3109/09638288.2010.535090.

Zanon, C., Bastianello, M. R., Pacico, J. C., & Hutz, C. S. (2014). The importance of personality and parental styles on optimism in adolescents. *The Spanish Journal of Psychology*, *17*(June 2015), E47. doi: 10.1017/sjp.2014.49.

Rachmat Mulyono[1], Yufiarti[2], and Elindra Yetti[3]

Effects of Parental Involvement and Child's Self-Regulation on Tolerant Behavior in Early Childhood

Syarif Hidayatullah State Islamic University of Jakarta, Indonesia[1]
Jakarta State University, Indonesia[2,3]

Abstract. This study aims to analyze the effect of parental involvement and child's self-regulation on child's tolerant behavior using quantitative method with multiple correlation technique. Multiple Regression Analysis is used to examine the effect of parental involvement and child's self-regulation on child's tolerant behavior. By using purposive sampling, this study assigned 149 children (aged 5–6 years old) and their parents domiciled in Jakarta. The results are (1) there is no significant effect of parental involvement on the child's tolerant behavior; (2) there is a significant effect of child's self-regulation on the child's tolerant behavior; and (3) parental involvement and child's self-regulation jointly affect child's tolerant behavior significantly. Therefore, the improvement of child's tolerant behavior can be achieved properly if there is a strong influence on child's self-regulation since early childhood.

Keywords: Tolerant behavior, parental involvement, self-regulation

1 Introduction

Indonesia is a diverse country. Ironically, one of the main issues among Indonesian people is the attitude of mutual disrespect and dishonor known as intolerant attitude (Syam, 2009). Intolerant behavior is not only a common phenomenon among adults but also an issue for children. In early childhood stage, especially in kindergarten schools, intolerant behavior can be seen from the children's lunch. Some children bring a luxurious food, but many children still bring simple food. There are even some children who only eat cakes (Sipa, 2016). Intolerant behavior in this case will not be raised if the teachers have cultivated tolerant behavior in the early age. Thus, the children will see the differences not as an obstacle in establishing a relationship with friends but as a cultural diversity that they must be grateful for (Sipa, 2016). As the consequences of intolerant behavior, children lack the adequate social skills to interact with others. In the other hand, socializing is a developmental task in the early childhood. If no one teaches the child to see and accept other people's differences, he will respond to these differences with fear and intimidation (Green, 2013).

Children should be introduced to the tolerance behavior at an early age, starting at four years old. The research by Burgess in 2004 showed that since one year old, the child's subconscious can absorb and reflect the behaviors of his parent and people around him. However, at the age of two and three years old, most of children tend to have an egocentric nature. Children assume that they are very special, so it is difficult for them to share and play with other people. When children reach the age of 4–5 years old, children are able to recognize social characteristics based on skin colors indicating that children begin to form stereotypes in certain groups (Burgess, 2004). The results of these studies also show that tolerant behavioral education can be introduced and developed in the early childhood.

Many previous studies that examine tolerant behavior (Menchik, 2014; Marsh et al., 2015; Arifin, 2010; Tonbuloglu, 2016; Assyaukanie, 2009; Abdullah, 2009; Alismail, 2016; Ratnawati, 2016; Sipa et al., 2016) are generally based on experimental research in improving tolerant behavior in children. However, research on factors that influence tolerant behavior in early childhood has never been conducted. Therefore, this research will fill such gap by finding and testing the factors that influence tolerant behavior in the early childhood. The factors that will be examined in this study are parental involvement and children's self-regulation.

Many prior studies provided general overviews on intolerant behavior concept aiming to increase tolerant behavior, mostly in education field. This study is different with previous studies in its method in examining intolerant behavior using empiric measures done by teachers at school emphasizing on emotional and behavior aspects in developmental field. This study focused on "The Effect of Parental Involvement and Child's Self-regulation on Child's Tolerant Behavior". The research questions are as follows: (1) are there positive influences of parental involvement dimensions on tolerant behavior?, (2) are there positive influences of self-regulation dimension on tolerant behavior?, and (3) are there positive influences of both parental involvement and self-regulation dimensions on tolerant behavior. This research is expected to give benefits for science development both theoretically and practically in the field of education and early childhood development, especially the development of child-tolerant behavior.

The results of this study can be used for complementing and strengthening the early childhood education theory and can be used as a reference for further researches in PAUD (kindergarten) studies, especially in developing child-tolerant behavior. The results can also be used as a reference for educators and education personnels in overcoming children's development problems in PAUD. This study clarifies factors that directly influence children's tolerant behavior so that it can be used as a reference to overcome the problem. In addition, the results in this study can be used as a practical reference for educators and researchers in the field of early childhood development for developing child's tolerant behavior.

2 Literature Review

Parental involvement, which is a measurable synthesis adopted from McNeal (2014), Konstantia (2014), Reynolds, and Harvard Family Research Project (HFRP), is a score of all forms of parental participation in children's education that is able to harmonize education at home and at school in order to support a child's developmental aspects. Parental involvement dimensions are (1) parenting, (2) involvement of parents in school, and (3) involvement of parents at home.

Self-regulation, which is a measurable synthesis adopted from Miller and Brown, Friedman and Schustack, and Einsberg, is a score of an individual's ability to manage, direct, and adjust (1) behavior and (2) emotions according to their social environment. As Morrison (2012) stated, children with well-developed self-regulation will preserve positive relationship with others and adapt to their environment without great difficulties. This study covers both emotional and behavioral aspects, but it excludes the thinking process as an observational instrument since it is difficult to observe it on 5–6 years old children.

3 Method

This study used quantitative approach with multiple correlation techniques. This study tested the influence with Multiple Regression Analysis methods, and multiple regression analysis techniques were employed to test the effect of each variable and to analyze the relationship between the research variables.

3.1 Sample

The population in this study is kindergarten students aged 5–6 years old (TK B students) and their parents in the DKI Jakarta area. The sampling technique used in this study is Non-Probability technique meaning each member of the population does not have the same opportunity for being a sample. Purposive sampling technique determines the samples with special considerations including (1) the acceptance of all elements at the school as a research place, (2) having an adequate number of students who can support the research, (3) the teacher's participation in research process, and (4) the parent's participation in conducting research.

3.2 Measurement Tools

Based on the sampling technique above, six (6) Kindergartens (TK) are qualified as samples, namely: TKI Al-Ummahatush Sholihat, TKI Rambutan, TKI At-Tin, TKI Al-Abror, TK Ria Pembangunan, and Wardah PAUD. The respondents are 149 kindergarden students.

3.2.1 Questionnaire

The data was collected using attitude scale instruments with the following types: tolerant behavior, parents' involvement, and child's self-regulation. Tolerant behavior scale contained 31 items. The test result was 4 of the total items showing the value of r<0.1353. It was implied that 27 items were valid and eligible for measuring variable of tolerant behavior in children with alpha of 0.934. The scale contained a series of statements that test the child to display tolerant behavior as specified in the instrument grid. The scale was analyzed by using the CFA analysis through the Mplus application.

The scale to measure parent's involvement consisted of 29 item statements. It was found that 3 of the total items had value of r<0.1353. Therefore, only 26 items were valid to measure parents' involvement with alpha of 0.0867.

The observation on a child's self-regulation was employed using an attitude scale with 24 items. All items had values of r>0.1353. So, all items were valid to measure the child's self-regulation.

4 Results

The data was analyzed using multiple regression analysis technique, and the hypothesis was proved using SPSS 17 software. There are three things to be considered in regression analysis. First, the researcher should consider the R-Square value to find out how much percentage (%) of variance in DV is explained by IV. The R-Square value can be seen in the Table 1. Second, the researcher should look whether all IV simultaneously have a significant effect on DV or not. Third, the researcher should check the regression coefficient's significance of each IV.

Based on the column of significance ($p < 0.05$) in Table 2, the null hypothesis stating that there is no significant effect of all independent variables on tolerant behavior is rejected. Thus, there is a significant influence of parental involvement (parental involvement in school, parental involvement in care parenting,

Table 1. R-square DV Variance Explained by IV

Model	R	R Square	Adjusted R Square	Std. Error of the Estimate
Tolerant	.582[a]	.339	.316	8.10195

Predictors: (Constant), BEHAVIOR, SCHOOL, HOME, PARENTING, EMOTION

and parental involvement in the home) and self-regulation (controlling emotions and regulating behavior) on tolerant behavior.

Table 2. Overall Influence of IV on DV

Model		Unstandardized Coefficients		Standardized Coefficients	T	Sig.
		B	Std. Error	Beta		
1	(Constant)	34.633	6.104		5.674	.000
	SCHOOL	-.063	.083	-.060	-.754	.452
	PARENTING	-.083	.103	-.073	-.807	.421
	HOME	.035	.092	.033	.379	.705
	EMOTION	-.423	.154	-.350	-2.743	.007
	BEHAVIOR	.842	.129	.830	6.505	.000

Dependent Variable: TOLERANT

According to Table 2, the regression equation presents that behavior tolerant = 34,633 - 0.063 (school) - 0.083 (parenting) + 0.035 (home) - 0.423 (emotion) + 0.842 (behavior). From the regression equation, it is clear that the self-regulation variable has a significant influence on tolerant behavior. The relation of managing emotion variable towards tolerant behavior has regression coefficient of -0.423 and Sig = 0.007 (Sig <0.05). It implies that the managing emotion variable significantly influences tolerant behavior. The relation of governing behavior variable towards tolerant behavior has a regression coefficient of 0.842 and Sig = 0.000 (Sig <0.05). It means that behavior variable significantly influences tolerant behavior.

Table 3. Regression Coefficients of All IVs for DV

Model	R	R Square	Adjusted R Square	Std. Error of the Estimate	Change Statistics		
					R Square Change	F Change	Sig. F Change
SCHOOL	.094[a]	.009	.002	9.78617	.009	1.298	.256

Model	R	R Square	Adjusted R Square	Std. Error of the Estimate	Change Statistics		
					R Square Change	F Change	Sig. F Change
PARENTING	.115[b]	.013	.000	9.79797	.004	.646	.423
HOME	.152[c]	.023	.003	9.78134	.010	1.497	.223
EMOTION	.379[d]	.144	.120	9.19095	.120	20.227	.000
BEHAVIOR	.582[e]	.339	.316	8.10195	.196	42.312	.000

The data in Table 3 indicates that the variable of parents' involvement in schools contributes 0.9% to tolerant behavior. The contribution is not significant with *p*-value of 0.256 (>0.05). The variable of parents' involvement in parenting contributes 0.4% to tolerant behavior. The contribution is not significant with *p*-value of 0.423 (>0.05). Further, the variable of parents' involvement at home contributes 1.0% to tolerant behavior. The contribution is not significant with *p*-value of 0.223 (>0.05). In addition, managing emotions variable contributes 12.0% to tolerant behavior. The contribution is significant with *p*-value of 0.000 (<0.05). Last, behavioral regulating variable contributes 19.6% to tolerant behavior. The contribution is significant with value of $p = 0.000$ (<0.05).

5 Conclusion

This study proved that there is a jointly significant effect of parental involvement and children's self-regulation on child's tolerant behavior. However, respectively, parental involvement does not have a significant effect on child's tolerant behavior. Child's self-regulation has a significant influence on child's tolerant behavior. Managing emotions variable from child's self-regulation contributes 12.0% to child's tolerant behavior, while regulating behavior variable from child's self-regulation contributes 19.6% to child's tolerant behavior.

5.1 Parental Involvement Does Not Significantly Influence Tolerant Behavior

This study found that there is no significant effect between parental involvement (X1) and child's tolerant behavior (Y). Thus, in the context of this study, an increase in parental involvement would not have an impact on improving child's tolerant behavior. The first research hypothesis is rejected because of the involvement of parents in the low category with an average of 53.02%. This is, presumably, because the relationship of parental involvement with child-tolerant behavior in the context of this study differs from the theoretical framework that has been built. For example, parents' involvement in assisting children in learning as one of the items in this study does not necessarily mean that parents accompany children to learn. Therefore, children will directly have high tolerant behavior because of the involvement referred in this research including the involvement of people at home, at school, and in daily care.

This is in line with the previous research, conducted by Moore and Zaff (in Horowitz & Tinkew, 2007), which shows that high parental involvement with children is related to the level of low-risk behavior. In contrast, low parental involvement is associated with high-risk behavior leading to the conclusion that low involvement of parents can influence children's negative behaviors such as children's intolerant behavior.

5.2 Children's Self-regulation Has a Significant Influence on Tolerant Behavior

This study found that there is a significant effect of children's self-regulation (X2) on child's tolerant behavior (Y). Therefore, increasing children's self-regulation will give an impact on increasing children's tolerant behavior. Self-regulation is an independent behavior control in children to assert their understanding of social expectations. Self-control is the ability to block impulses and control a person's behavior in the absence of external control, which has been repeatedly related to conscience development measures, such as resisting temptation and correcting wrong actions (Papalia, 2009). The results of this study prove that there is a significant positive effect of children's self-regulation on child's tolerant behavior. Children's self-regulation is one of the factors that plays an important role to enable children to behave tolerantly in their environment. This is in line with the research of Schneider (2014) which shows that positive actions by increasing the students' learning intensity to reach learning achievements will produce higher self-regulated students. In short, positive actions taken by students will result in good self-regulation.

5.3 Parents' Involvement and Children's Self-regulation Jointly Have a Significant Effect on Tolerant Behavior

This study found that there is a significant effect of parental involvement (X1) and children's self-regulation (X2) on children's tolerant behavior (Y). The influence of X1 and X2 on Y is confirmed by the results of hypothesis testing proposed in this study. It is shown that the proportion of variance tolerant behavior described by all independent variables in this study is 0.339 or around 33.9%.

It means that independent variables in this study causes 33.9% of the variation in tolerant behavior variables, while the remaining 66.9% is affected by other variables outside this study. The significant F test results show significance of 0,000 or ($p < 0.05$) so that the null hypothesis which states that there is no significant influence of all independent variables on tolerant behavior is rejected. This means that there is a significant influence of parental involvement (parental involvement in school, parental involvement in care, and parental involvement in the home) and self-regulation (controlling emotions and regulating behavior) on tolerant behavior.

This is in line with a research conducted by Burgess (2004) which shows that when children are 4–5 years old, children are able to recognize social characteristics based on skin colors. It indicates that children begin to form stereotypes in certain groups. So, parents' involvement in children's life has greater influence on children's behavior and simultaneously cultivating control in themselves, especially for tolerant behavior.

6 Affiliations

1. Name:	Rachmat Mulyono
Institution:	Universitas Islam Negeri Syarif Hidayatullah Jakarta
Address:	Fakultas Psikologi, Jl. Kertamukti No. 5 Ciputat-Tangerang Selatan
E-mail:	rachmat.mulyono@uinjkt.ac.id

2. Name:	Yufiarti
Institution:	Universitas Negeri Jakarta
Address:	Gedung M Pascasarjana, Komplek Universitas Negeri Jakarta, Jalan Rawamangun Muka, Jakarta 13220.
E-mail:	yufiarti@unj.ac.id

3. Name:	Elindra Yetti

Institution: Universitas Negeri Jakarta
Address: Gedung M Pascasarjana, Komplek Universitas Negeri Jakarta, Jalan Rawamangun Muka, Jakarta 13220.
E-mail: elindrayettii@unj.ac.id

7 References

Abdullah, A. C. (2009). Multicultural education in early childhood: Issues and challenges. CICE Hiroshima University. *Journal of International Cooperation in Education, 12*(1), 159–175.

Alismail, H. A. (2016). Multicultural education: Teacher's perceptions and preparation. *Journal of Education and Practice. ISSN 2222-1735 (Paper) ISSN 2222-288X (Online), 7*(11), *2016. www.iiste.org*

Arifin, S. (2010). *Attitudes to human rights and freedom of religion or belief in indonesia.* Yogyakarta: Penerbit Kanisius.

Assyaukanie, L. (2009). Fatwa and violence in indonesia. *Journal of Religion and Society, 11*, 1–21. https://doi.org/http://hdl.handle.net/10504/64439

Burgess, K. D. Teaching tolerance: closing the book on hate. 2004 *Ebook* http://www.preschoolerstoday.com/resources/articles/tolerance.html

Doorn, M. V. (2012). Tolerance. *Sociopedia. Isa*, 1–15. Https://Doi.Org/10.1177/2056846012121

Green, P. (2018). *Teaching kids tolerance. http://www.wholefamily.com/aboutyourkids/children/prejudice.html* (diakses pada 28 November 2018)

Horowitz, A. J. B.-T. (2007). Building, engaging, and supporting family and parental involvement in out-of-school time programs. *Research to Results (Practitioner Insights), 16* (June).

Konstantia, K. (2014). The effect of parental involvement in educational process. *International Journal of Humanities Social Sciences and Education, 1*(7), 147.

Marsh, T. E. J., & Knaus, C. B. (2015). Fostering movements or silencing voices: school principals in egypt and south africa context of western-framed reforms conceptual approach critical multicultural leadership educational leadership as a compromised solution penalization of resistance discus. *International Journal of Multicultural Education, 17*(1), 188–210. Retrieved from https://files.eric.ed.gov/fulltext/EJ1104929.pdf

Menchik, Jeremy. (2014). Productive intolerance: godly nationalism in indonesia. *Comparative Studies in Society and History, 56*(3), 591–621.

McNeal, R. B. (2014). 06_Parent Involvement, academic achievement and the role of student attitudes and behaviors as mediators. *Universal Journal*

Of Educational Research, *2*(8), 564–576. Https://Doi.Org/10.13189/Ujer.2014.020805

Menchik, J. (2014). Productive intolerance: godly nationalism In Indonesia. *Comparative Studies in Society and History*, *56*(3), 591–621. Https://Doi.Org/10.1017/S0010417514000267

Papalia, D., & etc. a. (2008). *Human development (psikologi perkembangan).* in *Cetakan ke-1, edisi ke-9.* https://doi.org/10.1038/nature05019

Ratnawati, S. (2016). Penerapan kegiatan mendongeng dalam meningkatkan sikap toleransi pada anak usia 5-6 tahun di tk aba melati. *Journal PGSD FIP UNIMED*, *6*(2), 2016.

Schneider, M. K. (2014). Regulated learning in teacher education the significance of individual resources and learning behavior. *Australian Journal of Educational & Developmental Psychology*, (14), 2014, 144–158

Sipa, S. P., & Miranda, D. (2016). Upaya guru menumbuhkan sikap toleransi bagi anak usia dini. *Jurnal Pendidikan Dan Pembelajaran*, *5*(6), 1–11.

Syam, N. (2009). *Tantangan multikulturalisme indonesia: dari radikalisme menuju kebangsaan*. Yogyakarta: Kanisius.

Tonbuloglu, B., Aslan, D., & Aydin, H. (2016). Teachers' awareness of multicultural education and diversity in school settings. *Egitim Arastirmalari – Eurasian Journal of Educational Research*, (64), 1–28. https://doi.org/10.14689/ejer.64.1

Wilis Srisayekti, Efi Fitriana, Achmad Djunaidi, and Marisa F. Moeliono

The Association between Parental Bonding and Social Anxiety: Is It Mediated by Self-Construal?

Padjadjaran University, Indonesia

Abstract. Previous studies show that social anxiety is associated with parental bonding and self-construal. To further examine the association, this research aims to examine whether the association between parental bonding and social anxiety is mediated by individual's self-construal. This study involved 590 high school students between the age of 15–17 years old (M = 16.30; SD = 0.61), from two cities in West-Java Province, Indonesia Bandung (50.85%) and Garut (49.15%)—65% were females, 60% were Sundanese, and all of them were Moslems. For the data collection, researchers implemented the Liebowitz Social Anxiety Scale (LSAS), the Parental Bonding Inventory (PBI) for Father and Mother, and the Singelis Self-Construal Scale. In addition, researchers used a multiple regression to predict social anxiety as an outcome variable from all independent variables (care, overprotection father and mother, interdependent and independent self-construal) simultaneously. The LISREL 8.3 program was applied to test whether self-construal is a mediator variable between parental bonding and social anxiety. The results indicate that the association between parental bonding and social anxiety is not mediated by self-construal. The negative significant direct effects were found between parental bonding overprotection and social anxiety (father: β = -.31, p =. 05; mother: β = -.10, p =. 05). Meanwhile, negative associations were demonstrated (1) between parental bonding care and interdependent self-construal (father: β = -.19, p =. 05; mother: β = -.23, p =. 05) and (2) between independent self-construal and social anxiety (father: β = -.30, p =. 05; mother: β = -.30, p =. 05).

Keywords: Social-anxiety, parental-bonding, self-construal

1 Introduction

Social Anxiety Disorder (SAD) (also known as social phobia) is a common and debilitating disorder characterized by marked fear or anxiety about one or more social situations, in which the individual is exposed to possible scrutiny by others (American Psychiatric Association, 2013). It is mostly accompanied by excessive preoccupation with fears of rejection, criticism, or embarrassment by others.

SAD was found as one of the most common of all the anxiety disorders (National Collaborating Centre for Mental Health (UK, 2013) with the lifetime prevalence of 12% (Kessler, Berglund, Demler, Jin, Merikangas, & Walters, 2005). Some studies reported that the phenomenon of social anxiety was found in Indonesia (Vriends, Pfaltz, Novianti, & Hadiyono, 2013; Srisayekti, Hadi, Fitriana, Moeliono, Pebriyani, & Susanto, 2016; Srisayekti, Moeliono, Fitriana, Suparman, 2019). SAD was reported as one of the most common anxiety disorders among children and adolescents (Faravelli, 2000). Cases of SAD were also found to be persistent and increasing among adolescents. SAD influenced young people's functioning overall, in the context of school, social, family, and personal interactions (Beidel, Ferrell, Alfano, & Yaganeh, 2001). These negative effects of SAD urge researchers to further understand the underlying mechanism of SAD to support counseling and other intervention programs.

There has been no single mechanism to account for the development of SAD (Hidalgo, Barnett, & Davidson, 2001). The review, on the risk factors of the development of SAD, states that the parent–child relationship, also known as parenting, appears to be one of the contributors to the development and/or continuance of social anxiety of the children.

According to parenting styles studies, parental-rearing styles of overprotection, rejection, and lack of warmth are associated with Social Phobia or SAD. Specifically, pattern of maternal overprotection, paternal rejection, and lower emotional warmth is associated with SAD (Knappe, Beesdo, Fehm, & Lieb, 2012). Several studies demonstrate that there is a relationship between social anxiety and a parenting style, and this relationship is marked by overprotection (or high control) and low-warmth parenting. The studies were conducted in various age groups, and within both clinical and developmental areas of psychological study (e.g., Bruch, Heimberg, Berger, & Collins, 1989; Greco & Morris 2002; Lieb, Wittchen, Hofler, Fuetsch, Stein, & Merikangas, 2000; Wood, McLeod, Sigman, Wei-Chin, & Chu, 2003; Brook & Schmidt, 2008). Some studies also report that individuals with SAD perceived both of their parents as less caring, rejecting, and overprotective (Arrindell, Hanewald, & Kolk, 1989; Bruch & Heimberg, 1994; Lieb et al., 2000; Parker, 1979). Other results with other samples indicate that authoritative and permissive parenting styles tend to promote the development of social anxiety (Akinsola & Udoka, 2013; Yousaf, 2015). An association was revealed between child-rearing attitudes, such as emphasizing others' opinions and shame tactics for discipline, and social anxiety in children. Bonding characterized by emotionally distant and controlling behavior was reported to be found in American or social phobic western European parents (Leung, Heimberg, Holt, & Burch, 1994). Despite these findings, a little is known about the potential mediators of the relationship between parenting and social anxiety.

Self-construal might be one of the potential mediators that has been used to explore mediation. It explains that individuals may construe themselves differently, either more interdependent self-construal or more independent self-construal (Markus & Kitayama, 1991; 2010). According to Singelis (1994), these two images of self give different consequential influences on individuals' way of thinking and doing. The interdependent self-construal emphasizes the connectedness and interpersonal relations. Individuals with interdependent self-construal concern more about belief, connectedness with others, external features, belonging, ability to "read others' minds," and commitment to duties and obligations. On the other hand, the independent self-construal emphasizes separateness and uniqueness of individuals. People with independent self-construal concern more on internal ability, unique self, and direct communication, and focus more on self-interest (Markus & Kitayama, 1991; 2010; Singelis, 1994; Kitayama, Yanagisawa, Ito, Ueda, Uchida, & Abe, 2017). Some studies investigate the relationship between self-construal and parenting (e.g., Corapci, Benveniste, & Bilge, 2018; Oyserman, Bybee, Mowbray, & Kahng, 2004). However, one of the studies that examine the relationship between parenting and self-construal of a person with social anxiety was conducted by Li and Gong (2018).

Concerning parenting and self-construal, recent study by Li and Gong (2018) show that a salient parental role promotes an interdependent self-construal. Meanwhile, regarding self-construal and social anxiety, study by Vriends et al. (2013) on general population demonstrates that interdependent self-construal predicts higher score on social anxiety. The replication of this research was conducted with more participants from general population; however, it revealed that the independent self-construal negatively predicted social anxiety, while interdependent self-construal did not give any significant contribution to the development of social anxiety (Srisayekti et al., 2019). These limited and inconsistent findings have not given sufficient explanation yet, on whether and how self-construal mediates parenting and social anxiety. Therefore, this research will examine whether the association between parenting and social anxiety is mediated by self-construal.

2 Method

2.1 Participants

This research is a correlational study among parental bonding, self-construal, and social anxiety. It involved 590 high school students from general population, non-clinical, in two cities in West Java Province, Indonesia, i.e. Bandung

(50.85%) and Garut (49.15%). The majority of the students were females (65%), Sundanese (60%), and all of them were Moslems. They were between 15 and 17 years old (M = 16.30; SD = 0.61), the mean age of their fathers was 48.44 (SD = 6.07), and the mean age of their mothers was 44.78 (SD = 5.32). The participants were recruited according to the recommendation of the National and Political Unity Agency District of West Java. Written informed consent was obtained from the participants prior to data collection.

2.2 Measurement Tools

We used a paper-pencil questionnaire consisting of self-report measures for social anxiety, parental bonding, and self-construal. The procedure of translation–back translation (Werner & Campbell, 1970) was applied for the Indonesian version of the questionnaire.

2.2.1 Social Anxiety

The Liebowitz Social Anxiety Scale-Self Report/LSAS-SR (Liebowitz, 1987; Baker, Heinrichs, Kim, & Hofmann, 2002) was used to measure social anxiety. The LSAS that was developed by Liebowitz (1987) measures fear and avoidance of the individuals, in social and performance situations. The LSAS contains 24 items, in which 13 items are related to performance anxiety and 11 items are related to social interaction situations. Each of the item is provided by two 4-point Likert-type rating scales, in which scale one for the intensity of fear (0=None; 1=Mild; 2=Moderate; 3=Severe) and for the frequency of avoidance of the situation (0=Never; 1=Occasionally; 2=Often; 3=Usually). The participants were asked to rate each item for the fear and the avoidance he/she experiences in the given situations. Good psychometric properties had been found, both for the LSAS (which the clinician filled out the answers for the patient) and for the LSAS-SR (the self-report version of the LSAS) (Heimberg, Horner, Juster, Safren, Brown, Schneier, & Liebowitz, 1999; Fresco, Coles, Heimberg, Liebowitz, Hami, Stein, et al., 2001; Safren, Heimberg, Horner, Juster, Schneier, & Liebowitz, 1999). The coefficient Cronbach's alpha of the LSAS-SR in this research was.94. In this study we used the Indonesian version of LSAS-SR (LSAS-SR-Indonesia) (Srisayekti, Fitriana, & Moeliono, 2023).

2.2.2 Parenting (Parental Bonding)

Parental bonding is used in this research to measure parenting. The use of parental bonding was applied, for example, in the study of Spokas and Heimberg

(2009). This research used Parental Bonding Instrument (PBI) to measure parenting. The PBI was developed by Parker, Tupling, and Brown (1979; Moeliono and Srisayekti, 2010), and included two subscales, i.e. a parental warmth/care scale (care will be used in this research) and a parental control/overprotection scale (overprotection will be used in this research). The parental care scale measures two poles of parental emotional behavior. One pole measures parental emotional warmth and empathy, and the other pole measures emotional coldness, indifference, and neglect. Similarly, the overprotection scale measures two poles. One pole measures parental control, overprotection, and prevention of independent behavior, and the other pole measures parental allowance of independence and autonomy (Parker et al., 1979) and the Indonesian version of it was developed by Moeliono and Srisayekti (2010). PBI included two subscales, namely 'The PBI measures the participants'. The PBI measures the participants' perception towards parental attitudes and behaviors related to the scales of care and overprotection. The PBI contains 25 items, and the participants were asked to rate each item on how their parents' attitude or behavior was during their first 16 years of life. The items were rated on a 4-point Likert-type scale ranging from "very unlikely (1)" to "very likely (4)." The ratings for the mother and the father were made separately. The PBI had high internal consistency for both subscales, as demonstrated, both in clinical and non-clinical samples by Arrindell, Hanewald, and Kolk (1989); Brewin, Firth-Cozens, Furnham, and McManus (1992), as well as in non-clinical samples by Spokas and Heimberg (2009). Adequate test–retest reliability had been shown in an undergraduate sample conducted by Whisman and Kwon (1992, 3 months) and in a clinical sample conducted by Parker (1981, 9 weeks). The coefficient Cronbach's alpha of the PBI Scale in this research was.75 for the PBI Scale rated for father and. 71 for the PBI Scale rated for mother.

2.2.3 Self-Construal

The Singelis Self-Construal Scale (Singelis, 1994) was applied to measure self-construal of the participants. The scale was developed by Singelis (1994) and the Indonesian version of it was developed by Moeliono and Srisayekti (2010). This scale contains 24 items, in which 12 items measures independent self-construal, and the other 12 items measures interdependent self-construal. The participants were asked to rate each statement in a 7-point Likert-type scale (1 = "strongly disagree," 7 = "strongly agree"). Various studies report that the subscales have either acceptable internal consistency (Singelis, 1994; Singelis and Sharkey, 1995; Sato and McCann, 1997; Norasakkunkit and Kalick, 2002) or low reliability estimation (Okazaki, 2000; Levine, Bresnahan, Lapinski, Wittenbaum, Morinagashearman, Lee, et al., 2003). In this research, the coefficient Cronbach's alpha of the independent self-construal sub-scale was.70, while that of the interdependent self-construal sub-scale was.70.

2.2 Analysis

All statistical analyses used were based on score scales. Descriptive statistics, Pearson's correlation, and multiple regression analysis were implemented using SPSS Statistics V21 program. Multiple regression was applied in order to predict social anxiety as an outcome variable from all independent variables simultaneously (care, over-protective father and mother, interdependent and independent self-construal). The LISREL V8.3 program was employed to test whether self-construal was a mediator variable between parental bonding and social anxiety.

3 Results

3.1 Descriptive Statistics

Concerning social anxiety, the results showed that the tendency of the participants to avoid the situations was higher (avoidance, M = 1.03; SD =. 38) compared to the fear they experienced (fear, M =. 98; SD =. 44). The results of the self-construal demonstrated that the participants scored more on interdependent self-construal (M = 5.55; SD =. 71) compared to independent self-construal (M = 5.11; SD =. 71). Parental bonding of the participants to their father was marked more by overprotection (M = 1.86; SD =. 41) compared to care (M = 1.01; SD =. 54). Similarly, their parental bonding to their mother was marked more by overprotection (M = 1.73; SD =. 42) compared to care (M =. 65; SD =. 49).

3.1.1 Correlations among variables

The results on Table 1 demonstrated that the significant correlations were found between parental bonding care father and the interdependent self-construal (r = -.15, *p* =. 00), as well as between parental bonding care mother and the interdependent self-construal (r = -.22, *p* =. 00). Parental bonding overprotective father had a significant correlation with independent self-construal (r =. 08, *p* =. 04), and parental bonding care mother had a significant correlation with independent self-construal (r = -.09, *p* =. 02). Social anxiety had a significant correlation with parental bonding overprotective father (r = -.19, *p* =. 00), parental bonding overprotective mother (r = -.10, *p* =. 01), and independent self-construal (r = -.30,

p =. 00). overprotective mother had no correlation with independent self-construal (r = -.03, ns).

Table 1. Correlation Matrix and Descriptive Statistics

1	2	3	4	5	6	7	
Over protective father	-.05	1					
Care mother	.29**	-.08*	1				
Over protective mother	-.07	.54**	-.14**	1			
Interdependent	-.15**	-.01	-.22**	.01	1		
Independent	-.07	.08*	-.09*	.03	.32**	1	
Social anxiety	.03	-.19**	.01	-.10**	-.07	-.29**	1
Mean	1.01	1.86	.65	1.73	5.55	5.11	2.01
Standard deviation	.54	.49	1.73	.42	.71	.71	.75

Note: ** p <. 001; * p <. 05.

3.1.2 *Regression analyses*

Two regression analyses were conducted to predict social anxiety based on interdependent self-construal and independent self-construal, parental bonding care father and parental bonding overprotective father, parental bonding care mother, and parental bonding overprotective mother. Model 1 consisted of the interdependent self-construal and independent self-construal, parental bonding care father, and parental bonding overprotective father as the independent variables, and social anxiety as the dependent variable. The model as a whole accounted for 11.8% of the variance in social anxiety scores (F = 19.35, p =. 00). Model 2 consisted of interdependent self-construal and independent self-construal, parental bonding care mother and parental bonding overprotective mother as the independent variables, and social anxiety as the dependent variable. All independent variables accounted for 9.8% of the variance in social anxiety scores (F = 15.78, p =. 00).

3.1.4 *Test for mediation*

Figure 1 showed the results concerning the participants' parental bonding with their father. The results showed three significant direct effects, i.e. parental

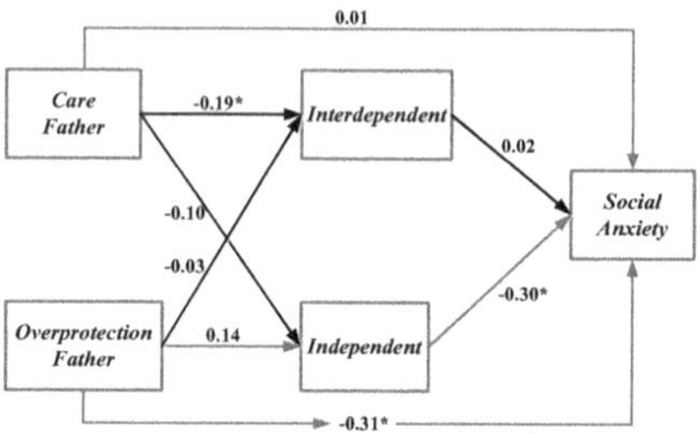

Figure 1. Relationships between Parental Bonding Father and Social Anxiety

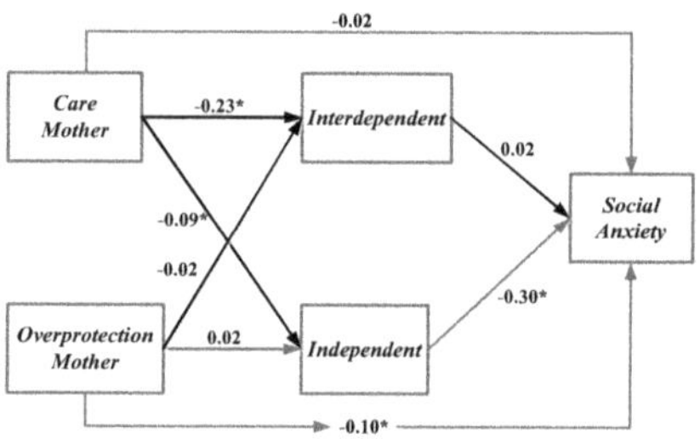

Figure 2. Relationships between Parental Bonding Mother and Social Anxiety
Note: * $p <. 05$.

bonding overprotective father to social anxiety ($\beta = -\ 31$), the parental bonding care father ($\beta = -\ 19$) to interdependent self-construal, and independent self-construal to social anxiety ($\beta = -\ 30$) These results give an understanding that the relationship between parental bonding father and social anxiety is not mediated by self-construal.

Figure 2 showed the results concerning the participants' parental bonding to their mother. The results demonstrated that parental bonding care mother had a significant direct effect on interdependent self-construal ($\beta = -\ 23$) and the independent self-construal ($\beta = -.\ 09$). Parental bonding overprotective mother had a significant direct effect on social anxiety ($\beta = -\ 10$), and independent self-construal had a significant direct effect on social anxiety ($\beta = -\ 30$). Based on these results, researchers can conclude that the independent self-construal could mediate the relationship between the parental bonding care mother and social anxiety ($\beta = -\ 03$). This research is a correlational study between parental bonding, self-construal, and social anxiety. However, it was not significant.

3.2 Discussion

Results indicated that there are significantly negative direct effects of parental bonding overprotection father as well as parental bonding overprotection mother on social anxiety. It gives an understanding that the participants' symptoms of the social anxiety are marked more by overprotective father and overprotective care mother. The explanation that clinging to parents (father and mother) for protection, which could result in greater parents' overprotection and control, and that these parents' reactions to increase protection could increase social anxiety (e.g. Spokas and Heimberg, 2009), could not be applied in this research. Contrarily, this research shows that the greater the participants clinging to their parents for protection, the less the social anxiety they experience. These negative associations are not in line with the results of previous studies, reporting that the marked overprotective parenting was significantly related to social anxiety (e.g., Lieb et al., 2000; Parker, 1979; Bruch et al., 1989; Arrindell, Hanewald, & Kolk, 1989; Bruch & Heimberg, 1994; Greco & Morris 2002, Knappe et al., 2012). The parents protection in the present study might give the individuals comfort that encourages them to have social experiences, and make them have less concerned about others' opinions (see Bruch, 1989; Bruch & Heimberg, parents' protection 1994). However, further research is needed to elaborate this explanation. All of the participants in this research were Moslems, who might be different from the participants of the previous studies, as it was not mentioned in the articles. It is then a question whether the Islamic values give any contribution to the findings. This might be a subject to explore in the next studies. Contribution of an ethnic group (e.g., the majority of ethnic group in this research was Sundanese), and the comparison between sex might also be interesting to investigate in the future studies.

There are results in this research that are in line with the findings of Srisayekti et al. (2019), i.e. (1) independent self-construal has a significantly negative association with social anxiety, and (2) the interdependent self-construal is not associated with social anxiety. These findings, however, are not in line with the findings of Vriends et al. (2013). These inconsistent results lead to a recommendation for future studies on the association between social anxiety and self-construal involving more participants from different regions with different ethnic groups in Indonesia.

Concerning self-construal, significantly negative associations were demonstrated (1) between parental bonding care and interdependent self-construal (father: β = -.19, p =. 05; mother: β = -.23, p =. 05) and (2) between independent self-construal and social anxiety (father: β = -.30, p =. 05; mother: β = -.30, p =. 05). Finally, the main results revealed that the association between parental bonding and social anxiety was not mediated by self-construal. These relatively new findings among previous studies concerning self-construal in relation to parenting and social anxiety, are introduced in this research.

It should be noted that the models in this research are based on the participants who construed themselves as more interdependent than independent and had stronger parental bonding overprotective father and overprotective mother (as compared to parental bonding care father and parental bonding care mother). The participants also reported that they have experienced mild to moderate social anxiety with a tendency to avoid social situation more than to experience fear.

The characteristics of the participants who were high school students, non-clinical, 65% female, and still lived with their parents might have contributed to the findings. The previous studies tried to relate these conditions to the conditions of the college students who mostly lived in their own rooms =/apartments and faced new socially and academically demanding situations (e.g., Spokas & Heimberg, 2009). Further studies on these variables could be conducted. Regarding methodology, the weaknesses of the PBI as a retrospective/recollecting self-report tool, that might be subject to memory bias, might be avoided in this research because the average age of the participants was 16.5 years old.

There are several limitations in this research. For statistical reasons, the findings of this research have to be considered with caution. The recruitment of the participants that was not by probability sampling contains a risk that the results are obtained just by chance. In this perspective, the results could only be seen in a descriptive manner and have to be treated as hypothesis-generating, not as confirmative results. Furthermore, the findings cannot be simply generalized to all students. Besides, the temporal primacy is lacking in the reports of the participants as the answers of the questionnaires were cross-sectional. The models in this research are based on the mild to moderate social anxiety experienced by the participants from general population and non-clinical samples. The application of the models on the clinical sample, therefore, is needed to be investigated further in the future studies.

4 Conclusion

The results of this research show that self-construal does not mediate the association between parental bonding and social anxiety. This is a new finding among the studies concerning self-construal in relation to parenting and to social anxiety.

5 Acknowledgments

The authors wish to thank the following institutions for the research funding: (1) the Ministry of Research, Technology and Higher Education of the Republic of Indonesia; (2) the Directorate Research and Community Service, for the data collection in Bandung; and (3) the Padjadjaran University (Academic Leadership Grant), for the data collection in Garut.

6 Affiliations

1. Name: Wilis Srisayekti
Institution: Padjadjaran University
Address: Jalan Raya Bandung-Sumedang km 21, Jatinangor-Bandung 45363
E-mail: wilis@unpad.ac.id

2. Name: Efi Fitriana
Institution: Padjadjaran University
Address: Jalan Raya Bandung-Sumedang km 21, Jatinangor-Bandung 45363
E-mail: efi.fitriana@unpad.ac.id

3. Name: Achmad Djunaidi
Institution: Padjadjaran University
Address: Jalan Raya Bandung-Sumedang km 21, Jatinangor-Bandung 45363
E-mail: a.djunaidi@unpad.ac.id

4. Name: Marisa Fransiska Moeliono
Institution: Padjadjaran University
Address: Jalan Raya Bandung-Sumedang km 21, Jatinangor-Bandung 45363

E-mail: m.fransiska@unpad.ac.id

7 References

Akinsola, E. F., & Udoka, P. A. (2013). Parental influence on social anxiety in children and adolescents: Its assessment and psychodrama. *Scientific Research,* 4(3A), 246–253. doi:10.4236/psych.2013.43A037..

American Psychiatric Association. (2013). *Diagnostic and statistical manual of mental disorders, DSM-5*. Washington, DC: American Psychiatric Publishing.

Arrindell, W. A., Hanewald, G. J., & Kolk, A. M. (1989). Crossnational constancy of dimensions of parental rearing style: The Dutch Version of the Parental Bonding Instrument (PBI). Personality and Individual Differences, 10(9), 949– 956. doi:10.1016/0191-8869(89)90059-7

Baker, S. L., Heinrichs, N., Kim, H. J., & Hofmann, S. G. (2002). The Liebowitz social anxiety scale as a self-report instrument: A preliminary psychometric analysis. Behaviour Research and Therapy, 40(6), 701–715. doi: 10.1016/s0005-7967(01)00060-2

Beidel, D. C., Ferrell, C., Alfano, C. A., & Yaganeh, R. (2001). The treatment of childhood social anxiety disorder. *Psychiatric Clinic of North America, 24*, 831–846.

Brewin, C. R., Firth-Cozens, J., Furnham, A., & McManus, C. (1992). Self- criticism in adulthood and recalled childhood experience. Journal of Ab- normal Psychology, 101(3), 561–566. doi:10.1037/0021-843X.101.3.561

Brook, C. A., & Schmidt, L. A. (2008). Social anxiety disorder: A review of environmental risk factors. Neuropsychiatric Disease and Treatment, 4(1), 123— 143. doi:10.2147/NDT.S1799

Bruch, M. A. (1989). Familial and developmental antecedents of social phobia: Issues and findings. *Clinical Psychology Review, 9*, 37–47.

Bruch, M. A., & Heimberg, R. G. (1994). Differences in perceptions of parental and personal characteristics between generalized and nongeneralized social phobics. *Journal of Anxiety Disorder, 8*, 155–168.

Bruch, M. A., Heimberg, R. G., Berger, P., & Collins, T. M. (1989). Social phobia and recollections of early parental and personal characteristics. *Anxiety Research, 2*, 57–65.

Corapci, F, Benveniste, H., & Bilge, S. (2018). Does Mothers' self-construal contribute to parenting beyond socioeconomic status and maternal efficacy? An exploratory study of Turkish Mothers. *Frontiers in Psychology, 9*, 1–11. https://doi:10.3389/fpsyg.2018.01245

Faravelli, C., Zucchi, T., Viviani, B., Salmoria, R., Perone, A., Paionni, A., Scarpato, A., Vigliaturo, D., Rosi, S., D'adamo, D., Bartolozzi, D., Cecchi, C., & Abrardi, L. (2000). Epidemiology of social phobia: a clinical approach. European Psychiatry, 15(1), 17–24. doi:10.1016/s0924-9338(00)00215-7.

Fresco, D. M., Coles, M. E., Heimberg, R. G., Liebowitz, M. R., Hami, S., Stein, M. B., et al. (2001). The Liebowitz Social Anxiety Scale: A comparison of the psychometric properties of self-report and clinician administered formats. Psychological Medicine, 31(6), 1025–1035. doi: 10.1017/s0033291701004056

Greco, L. A., & Morris, T. L. (2002). Paternal child-rearing style and child social anxiety: Investigation of child perceptions and actual father behavior. Journal of Psychopathology and Behavioral Assessment, 24, 259–267. doi:10.1023/A:1020779000183

Heimberg, R. G., Horner, K. J., Juster, H. R., Safren, S. A., Brown, E. J., Schneier, F. R., & Liebowitz, M. R. (1999). Psychometric properties of the Liebowitz Social Anxiety Scale. Psychological Medicine, 29(1), 199–212. doi: 10.1017/s0033291798007879

Hidalgo, R. B., Barnett, S. D., & Davidson, J. R. T. (2001). Social anxiety disorder in review: Two decades of progress. International Journal of Neuropsychophar- macology, 4(3), 279–298. doi: 10.1017/S1461145701002504

Kessler, R. C., Berglund, P., Demler, O., Jin, R., Merikangas, K. R., & Walters, E. E. (2005). Lifetime prevalence and age-of-onset distributions of DSM-IV disorders in the National Comorbidity Survey Replication. *Archives of General Psychiatry, 62*(6), 593–602. https://doi.org/10.1001/archpsyc.62.6.593

Kitayama, S., Yanagisawa, K., Ito, A., Ueda, R., Uchida, Y., & Abe, N. (2017). Reduced orbitofrontal cortical volume is associated with interdependent self-construal. *Proceedings of the National Academy of Sciences U.S.A., 114*, 7969–7974. doi: 10.1073/pnas.1704831114

Knappe, S., Beesdo, K. B., Fehm, L., & Lieb, R. (2012). Characterizing the association between and adolscent social phobia. *Journal of Anxiety Disorder, 26*, 608–616.

Leung, A. W., Heimberg, R. C., Holt, C. S., & Burch, M. A. (1994). Social naxiety and perception of early parenting among American, Chinese-Amercan, and social phobic samples. *Anxiety, 1*, 80–89.

Levine, T. R., Bresnahan, M. J., Lapinski, M. K., Wittenbaum, G. M., Morinagashearman, S., Lee, S. Y., et al. (2003). Self-construal scales lack validity. *Human Communication Research, 29*, 210–252.

Lieb, R., Wittchen, H. U., Hofler, M., Fuetsch, M., Stein, M. B., & Merikangas, K. R. (2000). Parental psychopathology, parenting styles, and the risk of social phobia in offspring. *Archives of General Psychiatry, 57*, 859–866. doi:10.1001/archpsyc.57.9.859

Liebowitz, M. R. (1987). Social phobia. *Modern Problems of Pharmacopsychiatry, 22*, 141–173.

Li, Y. J., & Gong, H. (2018). Being a parent together: Parental role salience promotes an interdependent self-construal. *Frontier in Psychology, 9*, 1462. doi: 10.3389/fpsyg.2018.01462

Markus, H. R., & Kitayama, S. (1991). Culture and the self: Implications for cognition, emotion, and motivation. *Psychological Review, 98*, 224-253. http://dx.doi.org/10.1037/0033-295X.98.2.224

Markus, H. R., & Kitayama, S. (2010). Cultures and selves: A cycle of mutual constitution. *Perspectives on Psychological Science, 5*(4), 420–430.

Moeliono, M. F., & Srisayekti, W. (2010). The Liebowitz Social Anxiety Scale (LSAS), Bahasa Indonesia version. Unpublished.

Moeliono, M. F., & Srisayekti, W. (2010). The Parental Bonding Instrument (PBI), Bahasa Indonesia version. Unpublished.

Moeliono, M. F., & Srisayekti, W. (2010). The Singelis self-construal scale, Bahasa Indonesia version. Unpublished.

National Collaborating Centre for Mental Health (UK). (2013). Social anxiety disorder: Recognition, assessment and treatment (NICE Clinical Guidelines, No. 159.). British Psychological Society. https://www.ncbi.nlm.nih.gov/books/NBK327674/. Accessed 27/ 01/2020.

Norasakkunkit, V., & Kalick, S. M. (2002). Culture, ethnicity, and emotional distress measures – The role of self-construal and self-enhancement. *Journal of Cross*-Cultural *Psychology, 33*, 56–70.

Okazaki, S. (2000). Asian American and white American differences on affective distress symptoms – Do symptom reports differ across reporting methods? *Journal of Cross-Cultural Psychology, 31*, 603–625.

Oyserman, B., Bybee, D., Mowbray, C., & Kahng, S. K. (2004). Parenting self-construals of mothers with a serious mental illness: Efficacy, burden, and personal growth. *Journal of Applied Social Psychology, 34*, 12, pp. 2503–2523. DOI: 10.1111/j.1559-1816.2004.tb01989.x

Parker, G. (1979). Reported parental characteristics of agoraphobics and social phobics. The *British Journal of Psychiatry, 135*, 555–560.

Parker, G. (1981). Parental reports of depressives: An investigation of several explanations. *Journal of Affective Disorders, 3*, 131–140. doi:10.1016/0165-0327(81)90038-0

Parker, G., Tupling, H., & Brown, L. B. (1979). A parental bonding instrument. The British *Journal of Medical Psychology, 52*, 1–11.

Rapee, R. M. (1997). Potential role of childrearing practices in the development of anxiety and depression. *Clinical Psychology Review, 17*, 47–67. doi:10.1016/S0272-7358(96)00040-2

Safren, S. A., Heimberg, R. G., Horner, K. J., Juster, H. R., Schneier, F. R., & Liebowitz, M. R. (1999). Factor structure of social fears: The Liebowitz Social Anxiety Scale. *Journal of Anxiety Disorders, 13*, 253–270. DOI: http://dx.doi.org/10.1016/S0887-6185(99)00003-1

Sato, T., & McCann, D. (1997). Vulnerability factors in depression: The facets of sociotropy and autonomy. *The Journal of Psychopathology and Behavioral Assessment, 19*, 41–62.

Singelis, T. M. (1994). The measurement of independent and interdependent self-construals. *Personality and Social Psychology Bulletin, 20*, 580–591.

Singelis, T. M., & Sharkey, W. F. (1995). Culture, self-construal, and embarrassability. *Journal of Cross-Cultural Psychology, 26*, 622–644.

Spokas, M., & Heimberg, R. G. (2009). Overprotective parenting, social anxiety, and external locus of control: Cross-sectional and longitudinal relationships. *Cognitive Therapy and Research, 33*, 543–551. DOI 10.1007/s10608-008-9227-5

Srisayekti, W., Hadi, S., Fitriana, E., Moeliono, M. F., Pebriyani, L. V., & Susanto, H. (2016). Kecemasan Sosial: Gambaran Deskriptif di Kota Bandung. Prosiding Seminar Nasional Hasil Penelitian dan Pengabdian Kepada Masyarakat, 43–46. Universitas Negeri Surabaya, 27 November 2016, Surabaya.

Srisayekti, W., Moeliono, M. F., Fitriana, E., & Suparman, Y. (2019). Kecemasan Sosial: Mengenal Fenomenanya di Indonesia. Bandung: Semiotika.

Vriends, N., Pfaltz, M. C., Novianti, P., & Hadiyono, J. (2013). Taijin kyofusho and social anxiety and their clinical relevance in Indonesia and Switzerland. *Frontiers in Psychology, 4*(3), 1–9. http://dx.doi.org/10.3389/fpsyg.2013.00003

Werner, O., & Campbell, D. (1970). Translating, working through interpreters and problem of decentering. In R. Naroll & R. Cohen (Eds.), *Handbook of Cultural Anthropology* (pp. 398–419). New York: American Museum of National History.

Whisman, M. A., & Kwon, P. (1992). Parental representations, cognitive distortions, and mild depression. *Cognitive Therapy and Research, 16*, 557–568. doi:10.1007/BF01175141

Wood, J. J., McLeod, B. D., Sigman, M., Wei-Chin, H., & Chu, B. C. (2003). Parenting and childhood anxiety: Theory, empirical findings, and future directions. *Journal of Child Psychology and Psychiatry, and Allied Disciplines, 44*, 134–151. doi:10.1111/1469-7610.00106

Yousaf, S. (2015). The relation between self-esteem, parenting style and social anxiety. *Journal of education and practice, 6*(1), 140–142.

Yufiarti, Meyke Garzia, Fellianti Muzdalifah, Erik

Effect of Positive Parenting on School Readiness in Early Childhood

State University of Jakarta, Indonesia

Abstract: This study aims to observe the positive parenting influence on school readiness in early childhood. This study is a quantitative descriptive research. The number of samples used by the researcher is 50 parents. The data was collected through questionnaires with Cluster Random Sampling technique. Moreover, the data processing and analysis techniques are descriptive statistics. The results of the study show that positive parenting support children's school readiness.

Keywords: Positive parenting, school readiness

1 Introduction

The success in achieving educational goals is largely determined by three factors which are the child's personal readiness, the parents' roles, and the school's roles. The purpose of education is to enable students to adapt well in various conditions so that children are able to survive in the future. In early childhood education, parents are the main educators in providing knowledge (insight) to their children. A parenting program may help parents to understand the good way in providing care to the children in accordance with the children's growth and development.

Being a parent gives joy, pride, and happiness in life. Many factors can be modified in order to influence child's development, and nothing is more important than the childcare quality. The need for a broad understanding on the fundamental role of parents is essential. For example, good parenting can stimulate development, well-being, and opportunities in a child's life. Parenting may help to improve the children's social and emotional development aspects that are needed when interacting with others including parents, siblings, family, peers, teachers, and so on. In addition, parenting also involves a number of interrelated and related functions such as child care, education, and socialization. An African proverb says, "It takes a village to raise a child." It can be implied that parents really need a strong community support in caring for children, for example, having a reliable partner or friend who gives moral support in raising children (Sanders & Turner, 2018).

Theoretically, parenting support through social interaction and positive behavior can be strengthened when the community fully participates in a parenting program. The importance of parenting as a whole can stimulate and improve some aspects in children's development and positively contribute to children's school readiness (Sanders, Burke, Prinz, & Morawska, 2017).

Family routines in parenting can prevent depression and anxiety in children who are preparing themselves for school (Fernando et al., 2018). Furthermore, the results of other similar studies explain that mental health, family factors, and parenting quality are the determinants in early childhood life. Therefore, positive parenting is very important for the children in their first five years, especially the parents' understanding of children's school readiness (Ryan, O'Farrelly, & Ramchandani, 2017).

2 Literature Review

2.1 School Readiness

School readiness is a complex concept. It covers not only the skills and abilities of reading, writing, and counting but also multidimensional concepts, including physical health and motor development, cognitive, social-emotional development, language, motivation, and attitude (Nurhayati, 2017).

Skills can help children in fulfilling school demands such as good working attitudes, and being able to concentrate, manage memories, and foster social relations (Peckham, 2017). Psychological readiness is closely related to child development aspects such as cognitive, language, social, self-emotional management, motor skills, and independence (Hurlock, 1997). In general, readiness to learn is the level of child development (of all ages) in which a child is ready to do or receive certain material learning (Lewitt & Baker, 1995).

From several explanations above, it can be synthesized that school readiness is the readiness to learn based on the maturity level of motoric, cognitive, language, social emotional development, self-discipline, and problem solving so that they are ready to do or receive certain material learning.

Preschool experience is designed to provide cognitive maturity aspects and social development during early childhood stages and aims to explore the ability in early childhood so that the children successfully pass the transition to school (Frederick Lunenburg, 2011).

The curriculum at an early age must provide a meaningful context for children. It shall not emphasize the difficult skill trainings (Lara Fridani dan APE Lestari, 2009). On the other hand, in the family environment, children get various skills, knowledge, values related to the needs in formal education (Kakia, Popov, & Arani, 2016). Some indicators of school readiness are as follows: (1) communication skills, (2) self-discipline, (3) basic thinking skills, (4) academic knowledge, (5) motoric physical development, and (6) social emotional maturity (Fayez, Ahmad, & Oliemat, 2016).

2.2 Positive Parenting

Positive parenting is a nurture based on love, mutual respect, warm relationships between children and parents, and children's growth stimulation. Positive care is done by prioritizing the appreciation, fulfillment, and protection of the rights and best interests of the child (Pendidikan et al., 2017).

It is important to support positive parenting. Many empirical studies and meta-analyzes prove the importance of positive care and security attachment in stimulating children's social emotional development (Anja Van Der Voort, 2018).

Positive parenting is an accurate observation on children's behavior and interpreting the children's willingness appropriately such as responding to the children's needs, for example, providing comfort when the child cries. VIPP-SD is one of the parenting programs that is able to increase positive parenting especially the sensitivity of parents so that it helps the relationship between parents and children, and it can reduce behavioral problems (Femmie Juffer, Estelle Struis, & Claudia Werner, 2017).

The main goals of positive parenting are (1) to improve the knowledge, abilities, and confidence of parents in parenting; (2) to provide care that is safe, pleasant, without physical violence, and create a safe environment for children; (3) to improve social, emotional, language, intellectual, and behavioral development through positive parenting practices (Sanders, 1999).

The basic principles of positive parenting consist of (1) ensuring a safe and engaging environment to support children's development and providing opportunities for children to explore and play; (2) creating a positive learning environment; (3) using assertive discipline by applying good and effective discipline such as not shouting, threatening, and using physical punishment; (4) having realistic expectation, beliefs, and assumptions about children's behavior in accordance with the stages of development; (5) taking care of one self as a parent, which means that parents must have a coping strategy for managing negative emotions such as depression, anger, anxiety, and stress (Sanders, 1999).

3 Method

This study is a quantitative descriptive research using a survey method. The research was conducted in Riau. The population of this research are 50 parents, and a questionnaire is used as the research instrument. The data analysis technique is descriptive statistics (percentages).

3.1 Samples

The sampling technique in this study is Cluster Random Sampling in which a researcher divides the population into separate groups known as clusters. In this technique, the researcher divided the population of parents into several groups or clusters based on their districts. Then the researcher selected several clusters through systematic random sample selection. Next, from the several sub-district clusters that had been randomly selected, the researcher decided to include all parents as the research samples for each district cluster through systematic random sampling.

3.2 Measurement Tools

The data collection tool in this study is a questionnaire. For positive parenting variables, this study uses the Likert scale (Often, Sometimes, Never), while for the school readiness variables, the researcher uses a Guttman scale (Yes, No).

3.1.1 Questionnaire 1

The positive parenting variables are measured by the questionnaire that consist of three indicators which are giving rewards, providing support in positive interactions, and being responsive to the child's cues and basic needs.

3.1.2 Questionnaire 2

The measurement of school readiness, as outlined in the questionnaire, is conducted based on Jordanian National Standards, namely the Community Attitude towards the Children's School Readiness (CARES), and the Arab Country has validated it as an Early Year Evaluation Tool (EYE). This instrument has been used universally with indicators such as academic knowledge, basic thinking skills, emotional social maturity, motoric physical development, self-discipline, and communication skills (Fayez et al., 2016).

4 Results

4.1 School Readiness in Early Childhood

Based on the instrument results using samples of 50 parents in Riau Province, it can be concluded that the parents who stated that their children were ready to attend school were 48 people. Furthermore, the parents who expressed that their children were not ready to go to school were 2 people. The data can be seen in Table1.

Tabel 1. School Readiness

		Frequency	Percent	Valid Percent	Cumulative Percent
Valid	No	2	4.0	4.0	4.0
	Yes	48	96.0	96.0	100.0
	Total	50	100.0	100.0	

The results of this study are supported by a research from Chang, Olson, Sameroff, and Sexton (2011). Their research explains that positive parenting can prevent deviant behavior during the transition from preschool to elementary school. The results of another research says that the relationship between parents and children is related to children's psychosocial and socio-emotional readiness (Anderson, 2016). This psychosocial and socio-emotional readiness are indicators of children's readiness to attend school.

4.1 Positive Parenting

Based on the research instrument which contained several positive parenting items, it was found that 2 parents stated "never," 38 parents stated "often," and 10 parents stated "sometimes" for giving positive parenting treatment to children. The data can be seen in the Table 2.

Tabel 2. Positive Parenting

		Frequency	Percent	Valid Percent	Cumulative Percent
Valid	Never	2	4.0	4.0	4.0
	Often	38	76.0	76.0	80.0
	Sometimes	10	20.0	20.0	100.0
	Total	50	100.0	100.0	

The results of this study indicate that 38 parents applied positive parenting. Based on the research results from Kiernan and Mensah (2011), positive care is a buffer between poverty and poor school performance. Positive parenting can reduce the risk of development delays in children. Children's social skills and behaviors, complex language development, and cognitive abilities may reduce the risk and affect the success of children in their future education (Williams, Asaolu, Cprek, Vanderpool, & Alexander, 2015).

5 Conclusion

It can be concluded that positive parenting has a positive impact on and contributes to school development and readiness aspects. Positive parenting characteristics can be seen from (1) ensuring a save and engaging environment, (2) creating a positive learning environment, (3) using assertive discipline, (4) having realistic expectation, and (5) taking care of one self as a parent. Thus, based on the data, it is implied that parents who apply positive parenting tend to have children who are ready for school.

6 Affiliations

1. Name:	Prof. Dr. Yufiarti, M.Psi.
Institution:	State University of Jakarta
Address:	Jl. Rawamangun Muka, Pulo Gadung, Kota Jakarta Timur, DKI Jakarta. Campus A
E-mail:	yufiarti@unj.ac.id

2. Name:	Meyke Garzia
Institution:	State University of Jakarta
Address:	Jl. Halimun Raya No.2, Kota Jakarta Selatan, DKI Jakarta. Campus D Psychology
E-mail:	meykegarzia@gmail.com

3. Name: Fellianti Muzdalifah
Institution: State University of Jakarta
Address: Jl. Halimun Raya No.2, Kota Jakarta Selatan, DKI Jakarta. Campus D Psychology
E-mail: f_muzdalifah@unj.ac.id

4. Name: Erik
Institution: State University of Jakarta
Address: Jl. Halimun Raya No.2, Kota Jakarta Selatan, DKI Jakarta. Campus D Psychology
E-mail: erik@unj.ac.id

7 References

Anderson, R. E. (2016). Focusing on family : Parent – Child relationships and school readiness among economically impoverised Black children. *The Journal of Negro Education*, *84*(3), 442–456. https://doi.org/10.7709/jnegroeducation.84.3.0442

Anja Van Der Voort, Juffer, F., & Bakermans-Kranenburg, M. J. (2018). Sensitive parenting is the foundation for secure attachment relationships and positive social – Emotional development of children. *Journal of Children's Services*, *9*(2), 1746–6660.

Chang, H., Olson, S. L., Sameroff, A. J., & Sexton, H. R. (2011). Child effortful control as a mediator of parenting practices on externalizing behavior: Evidence for a sex-differentiated pathway across the transition from preschool to school. *Journal of Abnormal Child Psychology*, *39*(1), 71–81. https://doi.org/10.1007/s10802-010-9437-7

Fayez, M., Ahmad, J. F., & Oliemat, E. (2016). Jordanian Kindergarten and 1st-Grade Teachers' beliefs about child-based dimensions of school readiness. *Journal of Research in Childhood Education*, *30*(3), 293–305. https://doi.org/10.1080/02568543.2016.1178195

Juffer, F., Struis, E., Werner, C., & Bakermans-Kranenburg, M. J. (2017). Effective preventive interventions to support parents of young children: Illustrations from the video-feedback intervention to promote positive parenting and sensitive discipline (VIPP-SD). *Jurnal of Prevention & Intervention in the Community*, *45*(3), 202–214.

Fernando, L. M. N., Sim, W. H., Jorm, A. F., Rapee, R., Lawrence, K. A., & Yap, M. B. H. (2018). Parenting Resilient Kids (PaRK), an online parenting program to prevent anxiety and depression problems in primary school-aged children: Study protocol for a randomised controlled trial. *Trials*, *19*(1), 1–12. https://doi.org/10.1186/s13063-018-2605-8

Frederick Lunenburg. (2011). Goal-Setting theory of motivation. *International Journal of Management, Business, and Administration*, *15*(1), 1–6. https://doi.org/10.1111/j.1551-2916.2010.04191.x

Hurlock, E. (1997). *Psikologi Perkembangan Suatu Pendekatan Sepanjang Rentang Kehidupan (Terjemahan)* (kelima). Jakarta: Erlangga.

Kakia, L., Popov, H. N., & Arani, A. M. (2016). A study of relationships between parents' and teachers' demographic factors and their judgments about children's activities and school readiness in primary schools of Tehran. *International Journal of Comparative Education and Development*, *18*(2), 100–119. https://doi.org/10.1108/ijced-10-2015-0006

Kiernan, K. E., & Mensah, F. K. (2011). Poverty, family resources and children's early educational attainment: The mediating role of parenting. *British Educational Research Journal*, *37*(2), 317–336. https://doi.org/10.1080/01411921003596911

Lara Fridani dan APE Lestari. (2009). *Inspiring education PAUD (Pendidikan Anak Usi Dini): Collection of True Stories*. Jakarta: PT Elex Media Komputindo.

Lewitt, E. M., & Baker, L. (1995). *School readiness. The future of children. Vol 5 No 2, Critical Issues for Children and Youths (Summer Autumn)*. Princeton University.

Nurhayati, W. (2017). Kesiapan Bersekolah di Indonesia, (20), 1–4.

Peckham, K. L. S. P. L. (2017). *Developing school readiness: Creating life long learners*. London.

Pendidikan, K., Kebudayaan, D. A. N., Jenderal, D., Anak, P., Dini, U., Pendidikan, D. A. N., … Keluarga, P. (2017). Pengasuhan positif.

Ryan, R., O'Farrelly, C., & Ramchandani, P. (2017). Parenting and child mental health. *London Journal of Primary Care*, *9*(6), 86–94. https://doi.org/10.1080/17571472.2017.1361630

Sanders, M. R. (1999). Triple P-Positive Parenting Program: Towards an empirically validated multilevel parenting and family support strategy for the prevention of behavior and emotional problems in children. *Clinical Child and Family Psychology Review*, *2*(2), 71–90. Retrieved from http://www.embase.com/search/results?subaction=viewrecord&from=export&id=L33445477

Sanders, M. R., Burke, K., Prinz, R. J., & Morawska, A. (2017). Achieving population-level change through a system-contextual approach to supporting competent parenting. *Clinical Child and Family Psychology Review, 20*(1), 36–44. https://doi.org/10.1007/s10567-017-0227-4

Sanders, M. R., & Turner, K. M. T. (2018). *Handbook of parenting and child development across the lifespan*. https://doi.org/10.1007/978-3-319-94598-9

Williams, C. M., Asaolu, I., Cprek, S. E., Vanderpool, R. C., & Alexander, L. A. (2015). Three positive parenting practices and their correlation with risk of childhood developmental, social, or behavioral delays: An analysis of the National Survey of Children's Health. *Maternal and Child Health Journal, 19*(11), 2403–2411. https://doi.org/10.1007/s10995-015-1759-1

Ditta Febrieta, Rohmawati, and Sulistia Aulia

Character Education for Adolescents as a Predictor of Social Sensitivity in the Digital Era

Universitas Bhayangkara Jakarta Raya, Indonesia

Abstract. Nowadays, the development of technology takes the people to the digital era. Millennials in their adolescence use gadgets for communicating, searching information, doing business, and even doing education courses. The digital era has both positive and negative impact. One of the negative impact is lack of social sensitivity which has begun to decrease because they prefer to communicate using gadgets by social media rather than face-to-face. Excessive use of gadgets by adolescents will potentially weaken their social skills. Social sensitivity is used by people to interact with each other in a community. Parents who teach character education to their children will enhance their social sensitivity. Therefore, character education plays an important role to control their attitude in the digital era. This study aims to determine the effect of character education given by family for adolescents towards the emergence of social sensitivity. Participants in this study were 261 adolescents in the age range 10–19 years old. The result revealed that character education gave effective contribution of 6.7% towards the emergence of social sensitivity.

Keywords: Adolescence, character education, digital era, family, social sensitivity

1 Introduction

Technology is growing rapidly nowadays. Everybody uses internet to do anything. Nowadays, millennials in their adolescence use gadgets for communicating, searching information, doing business, and even doing education courses. The APJII (2017) conducted a survey and revealed that internet users in Indonesia were 143.26 million people. Based on APJII's survey, most internet users are teenagers aged 13–18 years old. The survey showed that teens in millennial generation depend on gadgets. Gadgets facilitate people to communicate with the virtual world through applications such as WhatsApp, line, and Facebook messenger, and also give comments on Instagram social media, Facebook, twitter, and paths so that social interactions between them occur indirectly. The digital era now began to shift the culture and adolescents who have gadgets prefer to focus through these areas to access social media and interact with the virtual world rather than the real world. They are more concerned with the number of likes or comments on social media. Direct social interaction has become less due to the effects of social media development. Excessive use of gadgets causes adolescents to not care about situations that occur around them. They were reluctant to help or show concern whether verbal or nonverbal. Currently, the social sensitivity of adolescents has begun to decline due to the negative impact of the digital era. Adolescents who are sensitive to the social environment will not prioritize on their personal interests; they will be responsive, dare to act, dare to admit their mistakes, and also be responsible for their behavior. Tondok (2012) defined social sensitivity as the ability to react quickly and precisely to the situation.

Social sensitivity is a part of social skills that must be trained early through the smallest scope of individuals. So, the family has an important role in every child's growth from cognitive, affective, and social ----. According to Berkowitz (2002), families (especially parents) have a power to influence good character in children. Therefore, character education is believed to be something that can enhance social sensitivity in adolescents in the digital era. Character education intends to shape character based on values or norms in society (Kurniawan, 2015). The values given consist of components of the aspects of knowledge, feelings, and actions for oneself, society, and the nation (Afandi, 2011). The existence of character education given by parents to adolescents is expected to be able to increase the ability of children to interact socially in the digital era. As mentioned above, digital era has the negative impact social sensitivity. This skill begins to decline and affects social ability to interact with one another. On the other hand, character education can influence and even be predicted to improve social sensitivity. Based on these problems, this study aims to determine the effect of character education for adolescents towards the emergence of social sensitivity.

2 Literature Review

2.1 Social Sensitivity

According to Tondok (2012), social sensitivity is defined as a person's ability to react quickly and precisely to the social situation around them. Adolescents who have a social sensitivity can be responsive to the situation around them. They try to suit their attitude by norms in community that contain the concept of good, bad, inappropriate, or acceptable . Adolescents who are sensitive to social situations can read the situation and react appropriately to understand the situations that occur around them. They will try to be brave, be responsible for their actions, respect others, show empathy and sympathy, and also share with others.

Ningrum (2015) said that social sensitivity is an act that appears within the individual to feel the situation either happy or sad. If adolescents no longer care about their surroundings, they will be more concerned about themselves and their appearance on social media; this can be the indicator of weakened social sensitivity in adolescents.

Davis (1980) proposed three components to measure social sensitivity, namely perspective-taking behaviors emphasize non egocentric, fantasy, and empathic concern. Davis (1980) believes that perspective-taking is the tendency of individuals to take another person's perspective. Fantasy is described as the ability of individuals to change themselves imaginatively both in feeling and action through imaginary characters from novels, movies, or games . Empathic concern is part of social sensitivity that is an individual's ability to reflect feelings of warmth and sympathy related to caring for others .

2.2 Character Education

Character education is defined by Lickona as a deliberate attempt to make individuals understand, pay attention, and do the ethical values. Ethical values are important things to be taught to children from an early age. Berkowitz (2002) believes that families have an important role in develop character education in childhood. Giving character education to children is a planned effort carried out by various parties to build a character based on values or norms in the community . Additionally, Raharjo (2010) said that character education teaches the moral dimension and social environment as the basis for the formation of a quality generation. Character education is not only carried out by families but also carried out together and sustainably in the education field, and social environment.

To understand moral education, Lickona suggests that the moral education component can be divided into three main parts, namely: moral knowing, moral feeling, and moral action. Moral knowing as a form of moral knowledge, Lickona believes that individuals who have moral knowledge become the main foundation before individuals act. This moral knowledge is based on moral awareness, knowing moral values, being able to take other people's perspectives, moral reasoning, decision-making, and self-knowledge. Lickona said moral feeling is part of the feeling to behave based on conscience, self-esteem, empathy, loving the good, self-control, and humility, while moral action is part of the application of individual moral knowledge. Lickona believes to understand what drives a person to act morally, three things must be seen, namely: competence, will, and habits.

3 Method

Subjects in this study were adolescents in the age range of 10–19 years. Data is collected by purposive random sampling to match the characteristics of this study. The correlation and regression techniques are used in this study. Correlation techniques are used to determine the relationship between independent and dependent variables, and linear regression technique is used determine the effective contribution given by the dependent variable to the independent variable.

3.1 Sample

As mentioned in the Table 1, the sample in this study was 210 adolescents. Based on Santrock (2011) adolescents are from 10 years old to 22 years old. In this sample we found adolescents with an age range of 10–19 years. The majority of the characteristics in this study were girls with 159 (75.7%) subjects and boys with a total of 51 (24.3%) subjects. Based on age, the majority of the research subjects were in the age range of 14–16 years with a total of 124 subjects (59%), followed by the age range of 17–19 years with a total of 82 subjects (39%), and the lowest were subjects with ages 10–13 years with 4 subjects (1.9%).

Table 1. Sample Description

		Age			**Total**
		10 – 13	**14 – 16**	**17 – 19**	
Gender	Girls	3	92	64	159 (75.7%)
	Boys	0	32	19	51 (24.3%)
Total		3 (1.4%)	124 (59%)	83 (39.5%)	210 (100%)

3.1 Measurement Tools

3.2.1 Social sensitivity scale

Social sensitivity scale is composed and modificated from three components by Davis, namely: perspective-taking, fantasy, and emphatic concern. The scale consists of 12 items with each item in each component. Social sensitivity scale used Likert's model scale that moves from very inappropriate to very appropriate. Examples of items on this scale are like "Saya mudah menangis ketika melihat kejadian yang mengharukan." validation score is measured by content validity using discrimination item analysis. Azwar (2015) suggests the minimum score of validity is r 0.30 as valid item aitem. Based on that score, the validity score (r) on this scale moves from 0.417 to 0.639. Reliability score measured by internal consistency with the reliability score for this scale (α) is 0.781, means reliable enough to be used for research purpose .

3.2.2 Character education scale

Character education scale is composed and modificated from three components of education character by Lickona, namely: moral knowing, moral feeling, and moral action. The scale consists of seven items using a Likert's model scale that moves from very inappropriate to very appropriate. Examples of items on this scale are like "saya mempertimbangkan akibat dari perilaku yang saya lakukan." Validity score measured by coefficient total-aitem correlation. Azwar (2015) suggests the minimum score of validity is r 0.30 as valid item, and validity score (r) on this scale moves from 0.377 to 0.620 and the reliability score (α) is 0.530. Urbina suggests that for research purpose this scale cannot be used because reliability score (α) is below 0.60, means not reliable to be used for next research.

4 Results

4.1 Correlation Analysis

Bivariate correlation analysis is used to determine correlation between independent variables and dependent variables. The results of the Pearson correlation analysis can be seen in Table 2. Table 2 showed that coefficient correlation is 0.435 with a significance level of $p < 0.01$. It means that there is a positive relationship between character education and social sensitivity. A positive relationship on the correlation can be interpreted that there is a possible correlation between character education and social sensitivity in adolescents.

Table 2. Coefficient Correlation Analysis

		Character Education	Social Sensitivity
Character Education	Pearson Correlation	1	.435**
	Sig. (2-tailed)		.000
	N	210	210
Social Sensitivity	Pearson Correlation	.435**	1
	Sig. (2-tailed)	.000	
	N	210	210

**. Correlation is Determinant at the 0.01 level (2-tailed).

4.2 Regression Analysis

To determine the effective contribution of independent variables on the dependent variable, we used regression analysis. Table 3 revealed that F score = 48.423 with the significant level of $p < 0.001$. It means this model assumed to be linear regression analysis. Determinant correlation can be seen on R Square score of 0.189. These results indicate that character education made an effective contribution of 18.9% in the emergence of social sensitivity, and another 81.1% were influenced by other factors.

Based on Table 4, the regression equation can be interpreted that if there is no character education, then consistent score of social sensitivity owned by adolescents is 22.665. Meanwhile, if character education increase by 1%, it will increase social sensitivity by 23.525. The regression equation can be seen below:

$$Y' = a + b\,X \rightarrow Y' = 23.665 + 0.860\,X$$

Table 4. Coefficients

Coefficients[a]						
Model		**Unstandardized Coefficients**		**Standardized Coefficients**	**t**	**Sig.**
		B	**Std. Error**	**Beta**		
1	(Constant)	22.665	3.559		6.368	.000
	Character Education	.860	.124	.435	6.959	.000

a. Dependent Variable: Social Sensitivity

Based on the result of the t–test above, it can be seen that t score is of 6.959 with a significance value of $p < 0.001$. It can thus be interpreted from the hypothesis in this study that character education affects social sensitivity in adolescents. According to Berkowitz (2002), when children get older, school becomes more influential to give character education than family. Children will easily

Table 3. Regression Analysis

Model	**R**	**R Square**	**Anova Analysis**	
			F	**Sig. F**
1	.435[a]	.189	48.423	.000

a. Predictors: (Constant), character education

absorb moral learning, but adolescents nowadays face digital era where there is an influence of exposure to mass media, peer group, and community to behave morally. Therefore, mass media, peer groups, and community, as logical factors that cause character education, are less-determining factors in the emergence of social sensitivity in adolescents.

4.1 Comparative Analysis

T test and is used to find out the differences in each subjects' characteristics. Based on gender, there was no significant difference in character education ($p > 0.05$), but there was a significant difference in social sensitivity ($p < 0.05$). The mean difference showed that girls have a higher ability than boys to be socially sensitive (Table 5).

Table 5. T test Analysis

		Social sensitivity	Character education
T test		5.117	1.706
Sig.		0.000	0.092
Mean based on Gender	Girls	48.5912	28.8491
	Boys	43.0196	27.7451

Based on age groups (Table 6), significant differences were not found both in character education and social sensitivity ($p > 0.05$).

Table 6. ANOVA Analysis

		Social sensitivity	Character education
F test		2.677	2.858
Sig.		0.071	0.060
Mean based on Age Group	10–13 years old	40.5000	27.2500
	14–16 years old	47.8790	29.0645
	17–19 years old	46.5976	27.9146

5 Conclusion

Based on the results above, we found that character education has positive correlation with social sensitivity. Character education gave 18.9% effective contribution to social sensitivity. Girls have better social sensitivity than boys, and based on age group, significant differences not found both in character education and social sensitivity. For future studies, we suggest to consider forms of character education that fit to the adolescencts in the digital era and also consider other variables such as peer groups, mass media, and community.

6 Affiliations

1. Name: Ditta Febrieta
Institution: Universitas Bhayangkara Jakarta Raya
Address: Kampus II, Jln. Raya Perjuangan, Kota Bekasi, Indonesia
E-mail: ditta.febrieta@dsn.ubharajaya.ac.id

2. Name: Rohmawati
Institution: Universitas Bhayangkara Jakarta Raya
Address: Kampus II, Jln. Raya Perjuangan, Kota Bekasi, Indonesia
E-mail: rohmawati146@gmail.com

3. Name: Sulistia Aulia
Institution: Universitas Bhayangkara Jakarta Raya
Address: Kampus II, Jln. Raya Perjuangan, Kota Bekasi, Indonesia
E-mail: sulistyaaulia72@gmail.com

7 References

Afandi, R. (2011). Intgrasi pendidikan karakter dalam pembelajaran IPS di sekolah dasar. *Jurnal Pedagogia, 1*(1), 85–98.

Anggraini, K. C. (2015, Desember). Penerapan model pembelajaran inkuiri terbimbing untuk meningkatkan kepekaan sosial siswa dalam pembelajaran IPS di MTS Negeri Lamongan. *Akademika, 9*(2). Retrieved from shorturl.at/tvAR4

APJII. (2017). Infografis: Penetrasi dan perilaku pengguna internet Indonesia. Indonesia: TEKNOpRENEUR. Retrieved from file:///C:/Users/dita/Downloads/ZQoVUyKfuPblN9FrnRqvcAtixBdz1X.pdf

Aprinta, G., & Dwi, E. (2017). Hubungan penggunaan media sosial dengan tingkat kepekaan sosial di usia remaja. *The Messenger, 9*(1), 65–70.

Azwar, S. (2015). *Penyusunan skala psikologi.* Yogyakarta: Pustaka Pelajar.

Berkowitz, M. W. (2002). *The science of character education.* Stanford University: Hoover Press: Damon.

Davis, M. H. (1980). A multidimensional approach to individual differences in empathy. *JSAS Catalog of Selected Documents in Psychology*, 85.

Kurniawan, M. I. (2015). Tri pusat pendidikan sebagai sarana pendidikan karakter anak. *Jurnal Pedagogia, 4*(1).

Ningrum, D. I. (2015). Dampak penggunaan facebook terhadap kepekaan sosial peserta didik di SMPN 1 Demak. *Skripsi (Tidak Diterbitkan).*

Periantalo, J. (2015). *Penyusunan skala psikologi: Asyik, mudah, dan bermanfaat.* Yogyakarta: Pustaka Pelajar.

Raharjo, S. B. (2010, May). Pendidikan karakter sebagai upaya menciptakan akhlak mulia. *Jurnal Pendidikan dan Kebudayaan, 16*(3).

Santrock, J. W. (2011). *Perkembangan Anak* (7 ed., Vol. 2). Jakarta: Erlangga.

Setiawan, W. (2017). Era Digital dan Tantangannya. *Seminar Nasional Pendidikan.* Bandung: Universitas Pendidikan Indonesia.

Sudrajat, A. (2011, Oktober). Mengapa pendidkan karakter? *Jurnal Pendidikan Karakter, 1*(1).

Tondok, M. S. (2012). *Melatih Kepekaan Sosial Anak.* Surabaya: Harian Surabaya Post.

Rosleny Marliani[1], Anizar Rahayu[2], Zulmi Ramdani[3], and Feri Indra Irawan[4]

The Importance of Family Resilience in Islamic Context: A Thematic Content Analysis Approach

Universitas Islam Negeri Sunan Gunung Djati Bandung, Indonesia[1,3,4]
Universitas Persada Indonesia Y.A.I, Indonesia[2]

Abstract. Family, as explained in various literatures, has such a large function and role in the process of growth and development of physical and psychological aspects of an individual. Psychologically, intact family conditions involve emotional stability, thought clarity, good relationships, and spiritual maturity that are proportional among family members to form a model of a good family resilience. In the Islamic context, a study of family resilience is placed in an important position, especially in anticipating any stimulus that appears and how to transform the stimulus into a positive form. This study was conducted using a thematic content analysis (TCA) approach to 159 subjects consisting of a father, a mother, and a child in a family. The results of the exploration and the management categories in the open questionnaire proposed in the study illustrate a family resilience model based on Islamic approaches and perspectives. The specific factors that have a major influence on family resilience in this case include patience, gratitude, prayer, recitation, trust, worship, and *husnudzon* for all of the situations that afflict the family. The other results place the family resilience model as a life cycle in that if it is attached to these factors, family resilience becomes stronger.

Keywords: Family resilience, Islamic traits, thematic content analysis

1 Introduction

The family gives a big influence on the values and principles that are owned by the family members (Wu, Stephens, Du, & Wang, 2018). This important meaning becomes a foundation for people to learn and obtain values for their lives. Family is the first school for the formation of character and psychological development of a person (Luk et al., 2018), and the strength of a family is the foundation for the formation of a strong community. If a family could provide protection to every individual in it from a variety of negative things, social life would also be maintained (Marie & Mclanahan, 2012).

One of the reasons problems can occur in the family is because it does not have an effective family resilience, causing disharmony and imbalance in the family, and eventually leading to the emergence of ignorance between family members (Fitryasari, Yusuf, Nursalam, Tristiana, & Nihayati, 2018). In addition, many cases of depression that occur in the family are due to the function and role of family members that have not been well optimized allowing the problems to keep developing (Nam, Kim, DeVylder, & Song, 2016). Meanwhile, in Indonesia, cases illustrating other impacts of a low family resilience are showed, such as the increasing number of divorce cases and the psychological impact on all family members (Saidiyah & Julianto, 2016).

Spiritual well-being is an important condition and is a necessity for everyone in facing problems. This greatly determines how an individual is able to deal with his problem by always internalizing the beliefs and existence of higher substances outside himself that help them face life problems. According to Chang et al., (2012), spiritual well-being is considered the most decisive predictor of family resilience. Family members who are spiritually prosperous will spread enthusiasm and courage in facing life problems (Fehring & Rodriguez, 2013). This will also indirectly disseminate and strengthen the relationship between parents and children resulting in a stronger family resilience (Smith, Webber, & DeFrain, 2013). The relationship between spiritual well-being and resilience is associated with a positive relationship where reinforcement carried out regularly in the spiritual individual will have an impact on strength and resilience in social relationships, relationships between family members and friends, and life satisfaction (Smith et al., 2013). This research was conducted to explore the values of Islam that are relevant to the development process of family resilience and how these values become a positive alternative for families when facing various problems.

2 Literature Review

Resilience is defined as the capacity to recover from various difficulties faced and find alternatives to healthier ones (Walsh, 2006). In it, there is a process of fighting power, improving oneself, and growing in response to various crises and challenges faced (Walsh, 2006). According to Walsh (2006), the ability to anticipate crises and challenges can be perceived by each individual, depending on the size of the problems and the ability of the family to resolve them and empower all the resources they have. It is an active process in dealing with various problems, self-fulfillment, and growth in response to various crises and challenges (Walsh, 2006).

The term "family resilience" refers to a process of settlement and adaptation in the family as a functional unit (Walsh, 2006). This then becomes a perspective that is used to understand how families can be mediated in reducing stress and to overcome crises and prolonged problems. According to Patterson (2002), there are three most appropriate levels in understanding family as an important unit. First, family resilience must be understood as a way to get things that might be needed in a family. Second, there may be a number of possible risks that are directly related to the failure of the family to get what they expect. Third, family resilience is a need to understand protection mechanisms, such as what prevents the outcome of the process.

Islam views a family as a place where every member of the family is educated, nurtured, and strengthened in accordance with each psychological, physical, and spiritual elements. Individuals are born with a variety of potentials and strengths. These should be assets for them to be a decent human being (Abdullah, 2015). When individuals grow in strong families, all kinds of problems that may come into their lives can be effectively solved (Rahmanawati, 2019). A strong family in Islam is an achievement of a comprehensive and mutual understanding, mutual love, and becoming a moral compass for each other in all situations. Forming a harmonious family situation based on the values of kindness is considered capable in predicting the formation of strong family resilience (Manap et al., 2013; Marks, 2004; Stivens, 2006).

3 Method

This study uses a qualitative approach by focusing on the thematic content analysis (TCA) method. At this stage, data will be processed based on the results of an open questionnaire distributed to an intact family (a father, a mother, and a child). Researchers then conducted a detailed analysis based on predetermined themes and applied coding based on the data obtained (Roberts & Pettigrew, 2007; Vaismoradi, Turunen, & Bondas, 2013).

3.1 Sample

The population in this study are all families who still have complete members (a father, a mother, and a child) and live in the city of Bandung with a total sample of 159 families. Samples were selected using a purposive sampling technique in which subjects were chosen according to the characteristics determined by the researchers. Characteristics of the subjects are those individuals with families

Table 1. Open Questionnaire in Research (Modified by Walsh's (2003) and Fisher's (2010)*

No	Questions	Themes
1	Explain your family problem in daily live	Problem
2	Explain, how you cope your problem	Coping strategy
3	Tell us about your positive characters when facing problem	Positive character
4	Explain the role of each family members	Family members role
5	How about other family members in your family	Outside of nuclear amily
6	Explain the impact of religion and culture in your problem	Impact of culture and religion
7	Imagine, what a good family looks like	Ideal family

Note. Questions are made open in the form of a paper test to provide an opportunity for the subject to share his experience.

that are still intact (consisting of a father, a mother, and a child) who live in the area of Bandung and are Moslem.

3.1.1 Measurement Tools

Table1 is a list of questions used in the open questionnaires derived from Walsh's (2003) theory of family resilience and Fisher's (2010) spiritual welfare.

4 Results

The subjects involved in this study amounted to 159 people consisting of fathers, mothers, and children. Researchers carried out the research code of ethics in psychology and has received approval from the subjects when handing out the questionnaire. Below is the analysis result from the samples. Researchers applied a cognitive briefing, namely double crosschecking the results of the questionnaire then conducting objectification through a multi-judgment procedure (Ramdani, 2017; Ramdani, Supriyatin, & Susanti, 2018) to the subjects' answers.

Family resilience in the context of Islam is explained in a great detail through various mechanisms and approaches that are personal. The results of the study show that the most dominant thing done by the subjects when they are faced with family problems is by being patient. This is very much related to how they can survive and develop for the better. Other research conducted by Ramdani et al., (2018) already stressed that, by being patient, every problem faced by

Table 2. Sample of Subjects (Results by Respondent's Answers)

Subject	Description	Specific Factors
F1	"When faced with a problem I will usually be patient and still try to resolve it according to my ability. I will also draw closer to Allah SWT."	Be patient and draw closer to God
M3	"The teachings in Islam will always be used as family guidelines, I will try sincerely to receive and pray on every occasion."	Religion as a guide, Sincerity, and Prayer
C7	"I try to pray and believe that God will give the best results, after that do not forget to be grateful for what you have."	Prayer and gratitude
M9	"Patience and trust and often do self-reflection."	Patient and *tawakkal*
C11	"If there is a problem, you will usually try to be patient first, and believe that the problem will be resolved, and then try to think positively and not give up. and C (Child)"	Patient and *khusnudzon*
F15	"Be patient and thankful for what you have, the most important thing is to make use of our good potential and, with our strength, we must try to achieve the best."	Patience, gratitude, and self-reflection
M23	"If every problem faced is guided by religious rules and values, everything will be resolved properly, the most important thing is to introspect one another."	Religion is a guideline and self-reflection
C29	"Religion has always become a firm grip, thinking positively about problems faced in the family, and trying to be more mature towards what happens in the family."	*Khusnudzon* and potential to improve
F46	"The problem will be resolved if faced with a calm heart and clear mind, keep trying and be patient, and pray for one another."	Patient and prayer

Note. The symbol F (Father), M (Mother), and (Child), then continued with the sequence number of the subject in the study.

individuals, either personally or in groups, will be easier to deal with. Other results also assume that Islamic values built by an individual in a group will provide encouragement that strengthens other family members (Raus et al., 2013).

Islamic characters that are developed in the context of family resilience are increasingly typical to be seen if family members are consciously introspective and think positively in facing their problems (Salsabila, Rofifah, Natanael, &

Ramdani, 2019). This is then assumed to be the hallmark of the Muslim personality model which always studies the development of itself (Al-Karasneh & Saleh, 2010). After they realize that being patient, becoming closer to God, and carrying out positive activities are essential in overcoming their problems, they will look at their problems as media of learning (Helmy, Labib, & AbouKahf, 2014). Specifically, Islamic values will then be a reinforcement of the relationship between mentality of individuals in the family and the resolution of problems in their lives (Mohammad, Quoquab, & Omar, 2016) and will also form a characteristic for a problem-solving model in a Muslim individual (Hosseinkhanzadeh, Niyazi, Mosavi, & Zahedi, 2011).

5 Conclusion

Family resilience in the perspective of Islam is manifested in various factors that influence it including belief in God, gratitude, patience, and good prejudice to what happens (*husnudzon*). Thus, individuals who are able to strengthen various Islamic values within the family will at least have a strong family resilience. In the future, in order to objectify the results of this study, construction of family resilience–measurement tools in the perspective of Islam will be carried out with more respondents.

6 Affiliations

1. Name:	Rosleny Marliani
Institution:	UIN Sunan Gunung Djati Bandung
Address:	Jln. A.H. Nasution No 105 Kota Bandung
E-mail:	roslenymarliani@uinsgd.ac.id

2. Name:	Anizar Rahayu
Institution:	Universitas Persada Indonesia
Address:	Jln Diponegoro No 74 Jakarta Pusat
E-mail:	anizar.rahayu@upi-yai.ac.id

3. Name: Zulmi Ramdani
Institution: UIN Sunan Gunung Djati Bandung
Address: Jln. A.H. Nasution No 105 Kota Bandung
E-mail: zulmiramdani@uinsgd.ac.id

4. Name: Feri Indra Irawan
Institution: UIN Sunan Gunung Djati Bandung
Address: Jln. A.H. Nasution No 105 Kota Bandung
E-mail: feri.indra@uinsgd.ac.id

7 References

Abdullah, S. (2015). An Islamic perspective for strengths-based social work with Muslim clients. *Journal of Social Work Practice*, *29*(2), 163–172. https://doi.org/10.1080/02650533.2014.956304

Al-Karasneh, S. M., & Saleh, A. M. J. (2010). Islamic perspective of creativity: A model for teachers of social studies as leaders. *Procedia – Social and Behavioral Sciences*, *2*(2), 412–426. https://doi.org/10.1016/j.sbspro.2010.03.036

Chang, B. H., Stein, N. R., Trevino, K., Stewart, M., Hendricks, A., & Skarf, L. M. (2012). Spiritual needs and spiritual care for veterans at end of life and their families. *American Journal of Hospice and Palliative Medicine*, *29*(8), 610–617. https://doi.org/10.1177/1049909111434139

Fehring, R. J., & Rodriguez, D. (2013). Spiritual care of couples practicing natural family planning. *The Linacre Quarterly*, *80*(3), 225–238. https://doi.org/10.1179/0024363913Z.00000000023

Fisher, J. (2010). Development and application of a spiritual well-being questionnaire called SHALOM. *Religions*, *1*(1), 105–121. https://doi.org/10.3390/rel1010105

Fitryasari, R., Yusuf, A., Nursalam, Tristiana, R. D., & Nihayati, H. E. (2018). Family members' perspective of family Resilience's risk factors in taking care of schizophrenia patients. *International Journal of Nursing Sciences*, *5*(3), 255–261. https://doi.org/10.1016/j.ijnss.2018.06.002

Helmy, S., Labib, A., & AbouKahf, A. (2014). The impact of Islamic values on interpersonal relationship conflict management in Egyptian Business Organizations "an Applied Study." *Procedia – Social and Behavioral Sciences*, *143*, 1090–1110. https://doi.org/10.1016/j.sbspro.2014.07.561

Hosseinkhanzadeh, A. A., Niyazi, E., Mosavi, S. V., & Zahedi, M. (2011). Investigating the relationship between personality traits and problem-solving techniques in female college students with appropriate and inappropriate Hijab. *Procedia – Social and Behavioral Sciences*, *15*, 501–504. https://doi.org/10.1016/j.sbspro.2011.03.130

Luk, T. T., Wang, M. P., Leung, L. T., Chen, J., Wu, Y., Lam, T. H., & Ho, S. Y. (2018). Perceived family relationship quality and use of poly-tobacco products during early and late adolescence. *Addictive Behaviors*, *85*(January), 38–42. https://doi.org/10.1016/j.addbeh.2018.05.011

Manap, J. A. H., Noah, S. M., Kasan, H., Krauss, S. E., Mastor, K. A., Suandi, T., & Fazilah, I. (2013). The principles of Muslim religiosity and personality measurement. *Journal of Psychology and Human Development*, *1*(1), 36–43. https://doi.org/10.5964/ejop.v7i4.161

Marie, N., & Mclanahan, S. S. (2012). Family structure, parental practices and high school completion. *American Sociological Review*, *56*(3), 309–320.

Marks, L. (2004). Sacred practices in highly religious families. *Family Process*, *43*(2), 217–232.

Mohammad, J., Quoquab, F., & Omar, R. (2016). Factors affecting organizational citizenship behavior among Malaysian Bank Employees: The moderating role of Islamic Work Ethic. *Procedia – Social and Behavioral Sciences*, *224*(August 2015), 562–570. https://doi.org/10.1016/j.sbspro.2016.05.440

Nam, B., Kim, J. Y., DeVylder, J. E., & Song, A. (2016). Family functioning, resilience, and depression among North Korean refugees. *Psychiatry Research*, *245*, 451–457. https://doi.org/10.1016/j.psychres.2016.08.063

Patterson, J. M. (2002). Understanding family resilience. *Journal of Clinical Psychology*, *58*(3), 233–246. https://doi.org/10.1002/jclp.10019

Rahmanawati, F. Y. (2019). Building family resilience: A case study in a muslim family with autism child. *Proceeding ICOGISS*, 105–118. https://doi.org/.1037//0033-2909.I26.1.78

Ramdani, Z. (2017). Forgiving is not only forgetting (phenomenological study on forgiveness in individual who experiences a friendship conflict). *IJASOS-International E-Journal of Advances in Social Sciences*, *III*(9), 829–839. Retrieved from http://ijasos.ocerintjournals.org

Ramdani, Z., Supriyatin, T., & Susanti, S. (2018). Perumusan dan pengujian instrumen alat ukur kesabaran sebagai bentuk coping strategy. *Jurnal Psikologi Islam Dan Budaya*, *1*(2), 97–106.

Raus, N. M., Ghazali, N. M., Hassan, S. N. S., Jaafar, N., Tamuri, A. H., Muhamad, N. A. F., & Amat, R. A. M. @. (2013). The importance of self-efficacy: A need for Islamic Teachers as Murabbi. *Procedia – Social and Behavioral Sciences, 69*(Iceepsy), 359–366. https://doi.org/10.1016/j.sbspro.2012.11.421

Roberts, M., & Pettigrew, S. (2007). A thematic content analysis of children's food advertising. *International Journal of Advertising, 26*(3), 357–367. https://doi.org/10.1080/02650487.2007.11073018

Saidiyah, S., & Julianto, V. (2016). Problem Pernikahan Dan Strategi Penyelesaiannya : Studi Kasus Pada Pasangan Suami Istri Dengan Usia. *Jurnal Psikologi Undip, 15*(2), 124–133.

Salsabila, D. F., Rofifah, R., Natanael, Y., & Ramdani, Z. (2019). Uji Validitas Konstruk Indonesian-Psychological Measurement of Islamic Religiousness (I-PMIR). *Jurnal Psikologi Islam Dan Budaya, 2*(2), 1–10. https://doi.org/10.15575/jpib.v2i2.5494

Smith, L., Webber, R., & DeFrain, J. (2013). Spiritual well-being and its relationship to resilience in young people: A mixed methods case study. *SAGE Open, 3*(2), 1–16. https://doi.org/10.1177/2158244013485582

Stivens, M. (2006). "Family values" and Islamic revival: Gender, rights and state moral projects in Malaysia. *Women's Studies International Forum, 29*(4), 354–367. https://doi.org/10.1016/j.wsif.2006.05.007

Vaismoradi, M., Turunen, H., & Bondas, T. (2013). Content analysis and thematic analysis: Implications for conducting a qualitative descriptive study. *Nursing and Health Sciences, 15*(3), 398–405. https://doi.org/10.1111/nhs.12048

Walsh, F. (2003). Family resilience: A framework for. *Family Process, 42*(I), 1–18. https://doi.org/10.1111/j.1545-5300.2003.00001.x

Walsh, F. (2006a). *Strengthening family resilience.* New York: The Guilford Press.

Walsh, F. (2006b). *Strengthening family resilience.* New York: The Guilford Press.

Wu, W., Stephens, M., Du, M., & Wang, B. (2018). Homeownership, family composition and subjective wellbeing. *Cities*, (June), 0–1. https://doi.org/10.1016/j.cities.2018.07.004

Irwan Nuryana Kurniawan, Qurotul Uyun, and Resnia Novitasari

Islamic Premarital Education for Enhancing Marriage Readiness among Indonesian Muslim Emerging Adults

Universitas Islam Indonesia, Indonesia

Abstract. As the divorce trend among Indonesian Muslims continues to increase, it is highly important for families and stakeholders to find a more innovative and effective solution to minimize the risk of divorce and build a healthy marriage. Although research findings demonstrate a significant role of religion for determining marital quality, scientific evaluation of integrating Islamic values into family education programs to improve marriage readiness has not been widely practiced. This study examines the effectiveness of the Islamic Premarital Education to improve marriage readiness. To test the hypothesis confirming that marriage readiness after attending an Islamic-based family education program would be higher than before participating in the program, the present study used a repeated measurement design and involved 16 unmarried young adults (age range 19–31 years). The Marriage Readiness Scale (Ghalili, Etemadi, Ahmadi, Fatehizadeh, & Abedi, 2012), which revealed the mental readiness for marriage, moral readiness, emotional readiness, interpersonal readiness, and marital life skills was completed by each participant in the pre- and posttest assessment. The effect size estimate indicates that differences in marriage readiness created by the Islamic Premarital Education represent a large and substantive effect on improving marriage readiness of emerging adults in Indonesia. Implications for future programming and research are discussed.

Keywords: Islamic premarital education, marriage readiness, Indonesian Muslim emerging adults

1 Introduction

The increasing number of divorces in Indonesia (Cammack & Heaton, 2017; Hays, 2008; Pranawati, 2017; Rinaldo, n.d.) and research findings regarding the negative consequences of divorce (Amato, 2000; Amato & Cheadle, 2005; Amato & Keith, 1991; Clarke-Stewart & Brentano, 2006; Fagan & Churchill, 2012; Sands, Thompson, & Gaysina, 2017; Wallerstein & Lewis, 2004) suggest a very strong need for an empirically proven premarital educational program, which will improve the quality of marriage and in certain cases prevent distress and divorce

(Blanchard, Hawkins, & Fawcett, 2009; Carroll & Doherty, 2003; Fawcett, Hawkins, Blanchard, & Carroll, 2010; Halford & Bodenmann, 2013; Halford, Markman, Kling, & Stanley, Hawkins, Blanchard, Baldwin, & Fawcett, 2008; Hawkins & Ooms, 2012; Jakubowski, Milne, & Brunner, 2004). Simpson, Leonhardt, and dan Hawkins (2018) in their meta-analysis study found that relationship education programs have a medium effect on adolescents' and emerging adults' relationship knowledge, attitudes, and skills. According to Carroll et al., (2009), the conditions related to changes in relationship knowledge, attitudes, and skills are referred to as marriage readiness, specifically the process of developing interpersonal competencies, making a lifelong commitment, and gaining the capacity to care for others.

In contrast to previous studies (Hawkins et al., 2008; Wilmoth & Smyser, 2012), the Islamic Premarital Education is organized by a higher education institution and delivered by a trained professional psychologist. The education materials integrated with Islamic values contain knowledge about important skills and attitudes in building and maintaining healthy marriage relationships as well as overcoming common problems in marriages. To illustrate, premarital education among Orthodox Jews (Maybruch, Pirutinsky, & Pelcovitz, 2014), Christian premarital training (Marks, 2007), and the involvement of the Oklahoma clergy in marriage preparation (Wilmoth, 2005) significantly proved to be able to enhance marital stability as well as quality. These were identified as strategic approaches in the process of getting married. In the same way, the Islamic Premarital Education with a focus on Islamic religious approaches to marriage is also predicted to have a stronger influence on marriage readiness of Indonesian Muslim emerging adults, much higher than the influence level found in previous premarital education studies.

If the Islamic Premarital Education is found to be capable of facilitating marriage readiness of Indonesian Muslim emerging adults who are still single, the provision of such services can be a reliable choice to achieve its objective in improving the quality of future marital relationships and arguably preventing marital issues and divorce. This premarital education may more effectively help Indonesian Muslim emerging adults to form and sustain healthy marriages by preventing early relationship problems that shape negative future relationships.

This study investigates the effectiveness of the Islamic Premarital Education to enhance marriage readiness of Indonesian Muslim emerging adults.

2 Literature Review

The Islamic Premarital Education integrates research- and faith-based education specifically because the topic contents are based on the results of previous premarital education studies (Marks, 2007; Maybruch et al., 2014; Stanley, 2001) and, at the same time, takes into account the teachings of the Islamic faith regarding successful marriages (Asamarai, Solberg, & Solon, 2008; Bakar, 2010; Killawi et al., 2016, 2018; Syuqqah, 1999). It is designed through structured learning experiences: every week, participants attend two hours of lectures and one hour of small-group discussions with home assignments related to topics given at the end of the session. It contains three main topics that have been integrated with Islamic faith, namely, marriage commitment, marriage communication, and marriage conflict resolution.

When marital commitment is disrupted, participants of the Islamic Premarital Education will not easily break their marriage ties as they hold the firm belief that marriage is not only a commitment at the personal level (emotionally bound) and a social level (legally bound by state) but also a spiritual level (bound by Allah, a strong ethical commitment that is known in Islamic faith as *mitsaqan ghaliza*). This is a commitment that a husband and a wife are required to fulfill. Indeed, in the words of Allah Subahanu wa Ta'ala, "*O you believe, fill your covenants*" {Noble Qur'an, Chapter 4, Surah An-Nissa (The Women), Verse: 21}. Previous studies found greater sanctification of marriage correlated with marital satisfaction and with greater self-reported collaborative problem-solving skills to handle conflicts (Kusner, Mahoney, Pargament, & DeMaris, 2014; Mahoney et al., 1999).

Theoretically, assuming marriage has sacred qualities would motivate the participants of the Islamic Premarital Education program to manage conflicts well because the loss of their bond would entail relatively higher spiritual and psychological cost to themselves. The premarital education will help emerging adults to develop the knowledge and interpersonal skills that will strengthen their opportunities of experiencing a satisfying relationship and extracting themselves from a low-quality relationship. Furthermore, this equips Indonesian Muslim emerging adults with the ideas, tools, and practices on how to negotiate their relationships in Islamic ways that prepare them to achieve the happy as well as functional marriages and families that most of them aspire to have in the future. We hypothesize that emerging adults will demonstrate a higher marriage readiness score after participating in the Islamic Premarital Education program compared to before participation.

3 Method

The current study used a within-subjects design (Bellemare, Bissonnette, & Kröger, 2014; de Winter & Dodou, 2017) to evaluate the effectiveness of the Islamic Premarital Education to increase marriage readiness among Indonesian Muslim emerging adults. Marriage readiness was measured both before and after the premarital education was implemented. A within-subjects design was chosen because each subject serves as his/her own control, so the variability between subjects gets isolated and analysis can focus more precisely on the effects. In addition, a within-subjects design requires fewer participants since each subject is his/her own control and is cheaper to run.

The advantage of a within-subjects design is that the statistical power is usually higher than that of a between-subjects design, especially when the participants' scores for different conditions are correlated; that is, when participants are consistent with respect to themselves across different conditions. However, there are certain drawbacks associated with the use of a within-subjects design. One of these is that the results are susceptible to order effects, such as practice and fatigue, and to carryover effects.

3.1 Sample

Participant research recruitment is conducted by disseminating information about the need for research participants through bulletin boards on university campuses and through social media networks. A total of 16 study participants enrolled themselves voluntarily; participants were willing to commit to participating in all sessions of the Islamic Premarital Education and were included in the emerging adulthood stage. The age range of participants is between 19 and 31 years old, of which 62.5% are women and 37.5% are men (demonstrated in Table 1).

Table 1. Demographic Characteristics of Research Participants

Characteristic	**Total sample**
Gender	16
n	37.50%
% Male	62.50%
% Female	
Age	22.18± *3.71*
Mean ± SD	19.00–31.00
Min–Max	20.00
Median	

Characteristic	Total sample
Undergraduate study program	56.25%
% Psychology	31.25%
% Social science	12.50%
% Natural science	

3.2 Measurement Tools

Marriage readiness data were measured using the Marriage Readiness Scale (Ghalili et al., 2012) consisting of 20 items with Cronbach ∞ = 0.872, which revealed the mental readiness for marriage, moral readiness, emotional readiness, interpersonal readiness, and marital life skills. Participants were asked to rate each of the 20 marriage readiness behavior indicators listed using a 5-point Likert scale ranging from 1 (*Never*) to 5 (*Always*).

4 Results

The results, as shown in Table 2, indicate that there was a significant difference at $p = 0.05$ level in marriage readiness (t (15) = 2.82), and effect size estimate represents a significant effect of the Islamic Premarital Education on marriage readiness among Indonesian Muslim emerging adults. Strong evidence of the influence of the premarital education on marriage readiness can also be found in the estimated effect size, which includes (1) a large effect category for expressing feelings in close relationships and having good control of emotions, and (2) a medium effect category for having a positive outlook on marriage and family, having a logical expectation on marriage and partner, and not avoiding responsibility.

Table 2. Marriage Readiness and Its Behavior Indicators of Indonesian Muslim Emerging Adults

Variable/Behavior Indicator	Conditions		t(df), sig	Effect Size	
	Pre	Post		r** (%)	category
Marriage readiness	Mean = 4.00 SD = 0.38	Mean = 4.26 SD = 0.36	t (15) = 2.82*	r = 0.596 (35.63%)	Large effect
Expressing feelings in close relationships	*M = 3.8,* *SD = 0.88*	*M = 4.43* *SD = 0.51*	t (15) = 2.334*	r = 0.516 (26.64%)	Large effect
Having good control of his/her emotions	*M=4.06* *SD=0.68*	*M=4.50* *SD=0.63*	t (15) = 2.406*	r = 0.527 (27.84%)	Large effect

Variable/Behavior Indicator	Conditions		t(df), sig	Effect Size	
	Pre	Post		r** (%)	category
Having a positive outlook on marriage and family	*M=4.62* *SD=0.50*	*M=4.87* *SD=0.34*	t (15) = 2.236*	r = 0.499 (24.99%)	Medium effect
Having a logical expectation of marriage and partner	*M=3.93* *SD=1.18*	*M=4.43* *SD=0.62*	t (15) = 2.236*	r = 0.499 (24.99%)	Medium effect
Doesn't avoid responsibility	*M=4.50* *SD=0.51*	*M=4.81* *SD=0.40*	t (15) = 2.076*	r = 0.472 (22.31%)	Medium effect

* Significant at level 0.05 ** r represents effect size measure. According to Cohen (1992), the effect size is low if the value of *r* varies around 0.1, medium if *r* varies around 0.3, and large if *r* varies more than 0.5.

These findings confirm that integrating religious values has shown to substantively increase the magnitude of the Islamic Premarital Education influence (large effect size) on marriage readiness of emerging adults compared to previous meta-analysis studies (Simpson et al., 2018), which showed the influence of premarital education without incorporating a religious approach in the medium effect size category. In a broader context, the current research findings support the previous studies that demonstrated the positive impacts of religion and relational spirituality on marriage life (Ellison, Burdette, & Wilcox, 2010; Ellison, Henderson, Glenn, & Harkrider, 2011; Fincham & Beach, 2014; Fincham, Lambert, & Beach, 2010; Mahoney, 2000; McDonald et al., 2018).

In order to examine each indicator, it is shown in Table 2 that spirituality has an important role for enhancing emotional disclosure. It is related with previous research from Padgett, Mahoney, Pargament, and DeMaris (2019), who found that spirituality has helped couples to struggle and overcome difficult situations. It also enhances emotional expressions within adverse situations, thereby helping married couples to cope and build stronger bonds. Moreover, spirituality also helps an individual to achieve emotional control. This finding also correlates with other studies showing that religiosity helps individuals regulate their emotions using positive outcome strategies (Vishkin et al., 2019).

The current study findings should be considered with caution because there is (a) no counterbalancing to control order and carryover effects by letting participants undergo various conditions in different orders–future research should ideally use longitudinal design to trace the long-term effectiveness of Islamic Premarital Education, and (b) the study relied solely on self-reporting–future research should ideally include a standardized observational procedure.

5 Conclusion

Despite its limitations, this work offers valuable insights into premarital education regarding the role that religious approach may play in enhancing marriage readiness of Indonesian Muslim emerging adults.

6 Affiliations

1. Name: Irwan Nuryana Kurniawan
Institution: Universitas Islam Indonesia, Indonesia
Address: Yogyakarta, Indonesia
E-mail: kurniawan-in@uii.ac.id

2. Name: Qurotul Uyun
Institution: Universitas Islam Indonesia, Indonesia
Address: Yogyakarta, Indonesia
E-mail: qurotul.uyun@uii.ac.id

3. Name: Resnia Novitasari
Institution: Universitas Islam Indonesia, Indonesia
Address: Yogyakarta, Indonesia
E-mail: resnia.novitasari@uii.ac.id

7 References

Amato, P. R. (2000). The consequences of divorce for adults and children: An update. *Journal of Marriage and Family*, *62*(4), 1269–1287. https://doi.org/10.5559/di.23.1.01.

Amato, P. R., & Cheadle, J. (2005). The long reach of divorce: Divorce and child well-being across three generations. *Journal of Marriage and Family*, *67*(1), 191–206. https://doi.org/10.1111/j.0022-2445.2005.00014.x.

Amato, P. R., & Keith, B. (1991). Parental divorce and adult well-being: A meta-analysis. *Journal of Marriage and Family*, *53*(1), 43–58. https://doi.org/10.2307/353132.

Asamarai, L. A., Solberg, K. B., & Solon, P. C. (2008). The role of religiosity in Muslim spouse selection and its influence on marital satisfaction. *Journal of Muslim Mental Health*, *3*(1), 37–52. https://doi.org/10.1080/1556490080 2006459.

Bakar, O. (2010, December 13–14). *Family as a concept and as an institution in Islamic social thought: A theological-philosophical perspective* [Paper presentation]. International Conference on the Family Institution in the 21st Century – Ideals and Realities: IAIS, Kualalumpur, Malaysia. https://iais.org.my/attach/ppts/13DEC2010/ Osman% 20Bakar.pdf

Bellemare, C., Bissonnette, L., & Kröger, S. (2014). Statistical power of within and between-subjects designs in economic experiments.

Blanchard, V., Hawkins, A. J., & Fawcett, E. B. (2009). Investigating the effects of marriage and relationship education on couples' communication skills: A meta-analytic study. *Journal of Family Psychology*, *23*(2), 203–214. https://doi.org/10.1037/a0015211.

Cammack, M., & Heaton, T. B. (2017). Explaining the recent upturn in divorce in Indonesia: Developmental idealism and the effect of political change. *SSRN Electronic Journal*, *6*, 776–796. https://doi.org/10.2139/ssrn.2988407.

Carroll, J. S., Badger, S., Willoughby, B. J., Nelson, L. J., Madsen, S. D., & Mcnamara Barry, C. (2009). Ready or not? Criteria for marriage readiness among emerging adults. *Journal of Adolescent Research*, *24*(3), 349–375. https://doi.org/10.1177/0743558409334253.

Carroll, J. S., & Doherty, W. J. (2003). Evaluating the effectiveness of premarital education: A review of outcome research. *Family Relations*, *52*(2), 105–118. https://doi.org/10.1111/j.1741-3729.2003.00105.x.

Clarke-Stewart, A., & Brentano, C. (2006). *Divorce: Causes and consequences. Yale University Press* (Vol. 1). https://doi.org/10.1177/009430610703600418.

Cohen, J. (1992). A power primer. *Psychological Bulletin*, *112*(1), 155–159. https://doi.org/10.1037/0033-2909.112.1.155

de Winter, J. C., & Dodou, D. (2017). *Experimental design. In human subject research for engineers* (pp. 17–40). SpringerBriefs in applied sciences and technology. https://doi.org/10.1007/978-3-319-56964-2

Ellison, C. G., Burdette, A. M., & Wilcox, W. B. (2010). The couple that prays together: Race and ethnicity, religion, and relationship quality among working-age adults. *Journal of Marriage and Family*, *72*(4), 963–975. https://doi.org/10.1111/j.1741-3737.2010.00742.x.

Ellison, C. G., Henderson, A. K., Glenn, N. D., & Harkrider, K. E. (2011). Sanctification, stress, and marital Quality. *Family Relations*, *60*(4), 404–420. https://doi.org/10.1111/j.1741-3729.2011.00658.x

Fagan, P. F., & Churchill, A. (2012). The effects of divorce on children. Marriage and Religion Research Institute. Retrieved from https://downloads.frc.org/EF/EF12A22.pdf

Fawcett, E. B., Hawkins, A. J., Blanchard, V. L., & Carroll, J. S. (2010). Do premarital education programs really work? A meta-analytic study. *Family Relations*, *59*(3), 232–239. https://doi.org/10.1111/j.1741-3729.2010.00598.x.

Fincham, F. D., & Beach, S. R. H. (2014). I say a little prayer for you: Praying for partner increases commitment in romantic relationships. *Journal of Family Psychology*, *28*(5), 587–593. https://doi.org/10.1037/a0034999.

Fincham, F. D., Lambert, N. M., & Beach, S. R. H. (2010). Faith and unfaithfulness: Can praying for your partner reduce infidelity? *Journal of Personality and Social Psychology*, *99*(4), 649–659. https://doi.org/10.1037/a0019628.

Ghalili, Z., Etemadi, O., Ahmadi, S. A., Fatehizadeh, M., & Abedi, M. R. (2012). Marriage readiness criteria among young adults of Isfahan : A qualitative study. *Interdisciplinary Journal of Contemporary Research in Business*, *4*(4), 1076–1084.

Halford, W. K., & Bodenmann, G. (2013). Effects of relationship education on maintenance of couple relationship satisfaction. *Clinical Psychology Review*, *33*(4), 512–525. https://doi.org/10.1016/j.cpr.2013.02.001.

Halford, W. K., Markman, H. J., Kling, G. H., & Stanley, S. M. (2003). Best practice in couple relationship education. *Journal of Marital and Family Therapy*, *29*(3), 385–406. https://doi.org/10.1111/j.1752-0606.2003.tb01214.x.

Hawkins, A. J., Blanchard, V. L., Baldwin, S. A., & Fawcett, E. B. (2008). Does marriage and relationship education work? A meta-analytic study. Journal of Consulting and Clinical Psychology, 76(5), 723–734. https://doi.org/10.1037/a0012584

Hawkins, A. J., & Ooms, T. (2012). Can marriage and relationship education be an effective policy tool to help low-income couples form and sustain healthy marriages and relationships? A review of lessons learned. *Marriage and Family Review*, *48*(6), 524–554. https://doi.org/10.1080/01494929.2012.677751.

Hays, J. (2008). Marriage, poligamy, and divorce in Indonesia | Facts and Details.

Jakubowski, S. F., Milne, E. P., & Brunner, H. (2004). A review of empirically supported marital enrichment programs. *Family Relations*, *53*(5), 528–536. https://doi.org/10.1111/j.0197-6664.2004.00062.x.

Killawi, A., Daneshpour, M., Elmi, A., Dadras, I., Shamoon, Z., Elmi, A., … Nadir, Z. (2016). *Promoting healthy marriages and preventing divorce in the American Muslim community*. Washington, DC.

Killawi, A., Fathi, E., Dadras, I., Daneshpour, M., Elmi, A., & Altalib, H. (2018). Perceptions and experiences of marriage preparation among U.S.

Muslims: Multiple voices from the community. *Journal of Marital and Family Therapy*, *44*(1), 90–106. https://doi.org/10.1111/jmft.12233.

Kusner, K. G., Mahoney, A., Pargament, K. I., De Maris, A., & Demaris, A. (2014). Sanctification of marriage and spiritual intimacy predicting observed marital interactions across the transition to parenthood. *Journal of Family Psychology*, *28*(5), 604–614. https://doi.org/10.1037/a0036989.

Mahoney, A. (2000). Religion in families 1999 to 2009: A relational spirituality framework. *Journal of Marriage and Family*, *72*(4), 805–827. https://doi.org/10.1111/j.1741-3737.2010.00732.x.

Mahoney, A., Pargament, K. I., Jewell, T., Swank, A. B., Scott, E., Emery, E., & Rye, M. (1999). Marriage and the spiritual realm: The role of proximal and distal religious constructs in marital functioning. *Journal of Family Psychology*, *13*(3), 321–338. https://doi.org/10.1037/0893-3200.13.3.321.

Marks, J. P. (2007). *Christian premarital training in the local church setting: A study of the effectiveness of the Symbis Model in reducing divorce and producing stable and satisfying marital relationships.*

Maybruch, C., Pirutinsky, S., & Pelcovitz, D. (2014). Religious premarital education and marital quality within the Orthodox Jewish community. *Journal of Couple and Relationship Therapy*, *13*(4), 365–381. https://doi.org/10.1080/15332691.2014.953655.

McDonald, J. E., Olson, J. R., Lanning, A. H., Goddard, H. W., Marshall, J. P., Mcdonald, J. E., Marshall, J. P., & Empathy, S. (2018). Effects of religiosity, forgiveness, and spousal empathy on marital adjustment. *Marriage & Family Review*, *0*(0), 1–24. https://doi.org/10.1080/01494929.2017.1403992.

Padgett, E., Mahoney, A., Pargament, K. I., & DeMaris, A. (2019). Marital sanctification and spiritual intimacy predicting married couples' observed intimacy skills across the transition to Parenthood. *Religions*, *10*(3). https://doi.org/10.3390/rel10030177.

Pranawati, R. (2017). Changes in Muslim divorce mediation in Indonesia: A case study of the Yogyakarta Religious Court. *International Journal Of Indonesian Studies Issue*, (4), 31–52.

Rinaldo, R. (n.d.). Divorce in contemporary Indonesia 2017.09.21 | Center for Asian Studies | University of Colorado Boulder.

Sands, A., Thompson, E. J., & Gaysina, D. (2017). Long-term influences of parental divorce on offspring affective disorders: A systematic review and meta-analysis A R T I C L E I N F O. *Journal of Affective Disorders*, *218*, 105–114. https://doi.org/10.1016/j.jad.2017.04.015.

Simpson, D. M., Leonhardt, N. D., & Hawkins, A. J. (2018). Learning about love: A meta-analytic study of individually-oriented relationship education programs for adolescents and emerging adults. *Journal of Youth and Adolescence, 47*(3), 477–489. https://doi.org/10.1007/s10964-017-0725-1.

Stanley, S. M. (2001). Making a case for premarital education. *Family Relations, 50*(3), 272–280. https://doi.org/10.1111/j.1741-3729.2001.00272.x.

Syuqqah, A. H. M. A. (1999). *Kebebasan wanita: Pernikahan (Jilid 5)*. (E. Erinawati, Ed.) (2nd ed.). Jakarta: Gema Insani Press.

Vishkin, A., Bloom, P. B.-N., Schwartz, S. H., Solak, N., & Tamir, M. (2019). Religiosity and emotional regulation. *Journal of Cross-cultural Psychology, 50*(9), 1050–1074. https://doi.org/10.1177/0022022119880341.

Wallerstein, J. S., & Lewis, J. M. (2004). The unexpected legacy of divorce: Report of a 25-yearsStudy. *Psychoanalytic Psychology, 21*(3), 353–370. https://doi.org/10.1037/0736-9735.21.3.353.

Wilmoth, J. D. (2005). *Involvement of Oklahoma Clergy in providing marriage preparation*. Oklahoma State University.

Wilmoth, J. D., & Smyser, S. (2012). A national survey of marriage preparation provided by clergy. *Journal of Couple and Relationship Therapy, 11*(1), 69–85. https://doi.org/10.1080/15332691.2012.639705

Rika Fitriyana and Sarita Candra Merida

Preparing Parents in Facing Digital Era through Psycho-Education Program by Implementing Parenting Class at School: Life Skills to Prevent Negative Effect of Excessive Internet Use

Universitas Bhayangkara Jakarta Raya, Indonesia

Abstract. In the digital era, technology plays an essential role in everyday life. Most of the human activities depend on technology, such as working, studying, and even preparing meals. A survey conducted by the Indonesian Association for Internet Service Organizer (APJII) cooperate with technopreneur in 2017 found that in Indonesia, there were 143,26 million internet users, including children. Parents have a huge and very tough responsibility; they have to take proper care of their children's health, physical development, education, and intellectual affinities development. They are also responsible for better moral values, convictions, attitudes, and habits to a firm and well-behaved cultural relations in the family itself and the society where the child lives. Psychoeducation programs can help prevent the negative impact caused by excessive internet use and give parents knowledge about gadget management for children and how to handle gadgets and other multimedia problems. Through psychoeducation, parents will also learn new life skills to teach and handle their children to face the digital era's impact, especially excessive internet use. This research uses one group post-test design with descriptive analysis. This study's initial sample was 30 invited parents to a parenting class held by one of the Islamic schools in Bekasi but only 15 parents attending. Six parents leave the class when the session of knowledge is delivered. So, only nine parents complete all the sessions in parenting class. Based on the result, participants showed a better understanding of the impacts of excessive internet use and how to positively guide their children.

Keywords: Digital era, Internet, gadget, parents, psychoeducation

1 Introduction

In the world today, technology has grown so fast that affects most aspects of our life. In an era of global disruptions, knowledge and technology are vital factors. Challenges from various quarters are far more complex than we had to face 50 years ago (Sirisena, 2018). In Indonesia, a survey conducted by Indonesian Association for Internet Service Organizer (APJII), cooperate with technopreneur in 2017, found that in Indonesia, there were 143,26 million internet users, including children (APJII, 2017). Therefore, the internet plays a significant role in everyday life.

Digital transformation is the era we are facing right now, and it is quite challenging because it came with a great purpose, yet disrupting at the same time. In the past few years, excessive internet use leads to many mental health problems such as internet addiction (IA) and internet gaming disorder (IGD). Furthermore, since the impacts somehow bring damage to personality, mood, and creating low self-esteem in some cases, American Psychiatry Association (APA) included IA in Appendix III of the Diagnostic and Statistical Manual for Mental Disorders (DSM-5) as IG (Tripathi, 2017).

2 Literature Review

2.1. What Is the Disruption Era?

Before we discuss furthermore, it is crucial to know the definition of the disruption era itself. According to experts, the disruption era is updating the condition market, creating a new market, and updating and creating to follow technology development. Disruption is a developing technology with the growing technology application and change from to start-up. Disruption can become a threat or an opportunity for people. Through psychoeducation, the parents to increase self-disruption to face the disruption era. So, they ready to face the development of technology, change threats, or negative impact on opportunity, and further make it simple with the development of technology (Kasali, 2014).

2.2. What Is Internet Addiction

Internet is a new phenomenon that many practitioners are unaware of and consequently unprepared to treat. The best method clinically to detect compulsive use of the internet is to compare it with criteria for other established addictions as written in the Diagnostic and Statistical Manual of Mental Disorders (DSM-IV-TR). Prior research defined internet addiction as an impulse control disorder that does not entail an intoxicant (Sato, 2006).

According to Young et al., there are five subtypes of internet addiction based on different online activities. Those five subtypes are information overload, online gaming addictions, net compulsions, cyber-sexual addiction, and cyber-relationship addiction (Young, Pistner, O'Mara, & Buchanan, 2000).

Concerning gender and addiction, an exciting pattern of gender differences in addictive tendencies was reported by Greenberg et al. in their research about addictive behavior. Analysis of addiction's substances and activities found that men reported more significant addiction to cigarettes, alcohol, video games, gambling, and internet use (Greenberg, Lewis, & Dodd, 1999).

2.3. Is Psychoeducation

Psychoeducation has six aspects among teaching various life skills to the people, tend to experiential learning to teach something, humanistic approach, focus to more practice, and more significant scope than individual approach (Supratiknya, 2011). Psychoeducation is one of the method development programs for social life skills. Generally, psychoeducation teaches the people in the school, community, or other public areas. As for this research, it is taught to the parents at school. As many research found, parents play an essential role in children's development (Santrock, 2012).

The psychoeducation program was based on a literature review performed to determine the parents' problems when interacting with children in the digital era. A study conducted in Minnesota, USA, found that parenting programs significantly increased family and dyadic functioning and decreased child misbehavior reported by parents who attended this class (Berge, Law, Johnson, & Wells, 2013). Based on that, we tried to create a parenting program and applied it to our research. The psychoeducation program was based on a literature review performed to determine the parents' problems when interacting with children in the digital era.

Stages on psychoeducation program that we use in this research are similar to research conducted by Mcfarlane, Downing, and Dixon (2012) such as giving information about the program, the importance of psychoeducation, and to combine the information in several related areas such as cognitive, emotions, and how to manage the problem from psychoeducation material.

3 Method

This research uses a one-group post-test experimental design. Only one group is given manipulation, and after a certain period, the response is measured as a dependent variable (Seniati, Yulianto, & Setiadi, 2011). Using the one-group post-test-only design, a researcher measures a dependent variable for one group of participants following a treatment (Sage, 2019). The results are displayed on the table, and a descriptive analysis is shown to find behavior changes after attending the psychoeducation program.

Table 1. Psychoeducation Program

No.	Session	Topics	Learning Techniques	Durations
1.	Opening	Acquaintance, sharing of expectation about the program	Giving information, question-answer format, sharing emotions and experience	15 Minutes
2. .	Education Program	Facing the digital era: an era of disruption	Lecture, assignment, sharing session	20 Minutes
		Child development	Lecture, discussion	20 Minutes
		Internet addiction	Lecture, sharing session, assignment	20 Minutes
		Ways to handle the negative impact of excessive internet use	Discussion, sharing session	20 Minutes
3.	Closing	Assessment (post-test session)	Questionnaire	10 Minutes

This program was arranged according to psychoeducation theory from)

All of the respondents were parents with kids who went to the same school where this program was implemented. Parents were invited to join this program to help them deal with problems related to excessive internet use.

3.1 Sample

Sample for this research are parents attending parenting classes held by one of the Islamic school in Bekasi. The number of parents attending was 15 (n=15), but only nine completed the questionnaire after a session because six parents left the class when the material was delivered. For this research, this group is parents attending a parenting class. The treatment is psychoeducation with topics about gadget management for children and handling problems related to gadgets and other multimedia tools.

3.2 Measurement Tools

After providing the psychoeducation program, parents are given a questionnaire related to the topic of psychoeducation. It consists of a question about the parent's understanding of the topic that has been delivered before. The topics are internet addiction, gadget management, and how to handle the negative impact of excessive use of the internet. The time limit for answering is approximately 10 minutes after the treatment was given to avoid fake answering.

4 Results

Data for this research was collected through questionnaires filled by participants after they attended the psychoeducation program. After the questionnaire was collected, the researcher counted by using a tally. Lastly, the results were described using the table and also the narrative description.

Table 2. Post-test Result

No	Topics	Learning Techniques	Percentage (%)
1.	Acquaintance, sharing of expectation about the program	Giving information, question-answer format, sharing emotions and experience	85
2.	Facing the digital era: an era of disruption	Lecture, assignment	80
3.	Child development	Lecture, discussion	90
4.	Internet addiction	Lecture, sharing session, assignment	85
5.	Ways to handle the negative impact of excessive internet use	Discussion, sharing session	90

From the participant's post-test results, 85% gained new knowledge from parenting class, mainly how to deal with the gadgets. In the first session, the facilitator and participants stated their expectations about the program as part of the acquaintance. Psychoeducation program used various learning techniques, and in this session, the primary purpose was to give information and also sharing emotions and experiences among participants.

The second session topic was about facing the digital era, where technology became part of daily life activities. This session brought benefits and also danger at the same time. That is why the digital era is also known as the disruption era. Through the lecture, 80% of participants gained knowledge about the digital era, the disruption era, and how to manage gadget use positively. It helped parents to deal with children who have a problem with excessive use of the internet. They would practice it at home with their children, just like the simulation they had on this program.

The third session topic was child development, where parents were taught to increase their awareness due to things related such as physical, cognitive state, and also social-emotional development. Based on the test, 90% of participants managed to increase their awareness of child development and better understand their children.

In the fourth session, 85% of participants learned and discussed internet addiction from a mental health perspective. They realized the need to be careful in providing gadgets to children. They also started to recognize signs of internet addiction in children and how to prevent that from happening. Every parent has different ways; by sharing, they learned which ways were practical and easy to apply in real life.

In the last session, parents were taught how to make a plan to protect children from internet addiction. Making a plan would be easier for parents to implement it in real life for time management, positive reinforcement, negative impacts about using gadgets, and the importance of accompanying children while they used gadgets. The test result showed that 90% understood the topic very well.

Based on the result, participants understood the impacts of excessive internet use and how to guide their children in positive ways. Through the psychoeducation program, parents have a piece of new knowledge and skill for managing gadgets and handling the problems related to gadgets. After the psychoeducation has been delivered, parents plan to manage their children for using the gadget. A strategic plan would help parents be more disciplined in managing their children's habit of using the gadget.

5 Conclusion

This study confirmed that through the psychoeducation program, participants showed a better understanding of the impacts of excessive internet use and how to guide their children in positive ways. So these parents have a new point of view about manage their children using the gadget. Like the previous study of giving a brief, psychoeducation program can help the family with problems adapting to their environment. In this case, parents learn new ways to adapt to high technology, primarily related to internet use (Duran & Barlas, 2016). In this research, through a psychoeducation program, parents were given knowledge about gadget management for children and how to handle problems related to the gadget and other multimedia. After this program, parents get new knowledge for learning new life skills about teaching and handling their children to face the digital era's impact, especially excessive internet use. Similar to the research conducted by Torres-rodríguez, Griffiths, and Carbonell (2018), psychoeducation gives information to complete the previous information.

On the other hand, the research has limitations. Design one group only post-test design cannot be generalized in other populations because there is a factor influencing this research's internal validity, such as proactive history, retroactive history, and experimental mortality (Seniati, Yulianto, & Setiadi, 2011). Proactive and retroactive history is an experience or something that already exists in the participants participate in a similar workshop or seminar, educational background from the parents to get more information about how to handle using the gadget for upgrading knowledge about using the gadget for children.

6 Affiliations

1. Name:	Rika Fitriyana
Institution:	Faculty of Psychology, Universitas Bhayangkara Jakarta Raya
Address:	Kampus II Jl. Perjuangan Raya, Marga Mulya, Bekasi Utara Indonesia
E-mail:	rika.fitriyana@dsn.ubharajaya.ac.id

2. Name:	Sarita Candra Merida
Institution:	Faculty of Psychology, Universitas Bhayangkara Jakarta Raya
Address:	Kampus II Jl. Perjuangan Raya, Marga Mulya, Bekasi Utara Indonesia
E-mail:	sarita.candra@dsn.ubharajaya.ac.id

7 References

APJII. (2017). Penetrasi & Perilaku Pengguna Internet Indonesia 2017. Asosiasi Penyelenggara Jasa Internet Indonesia.

Berge, J., Law, D., Johnson, J., & Wells, M. (2013). NIH Public Access. *Families, Systems and Health*, *28*(3), 224–235. https://doi.org/10.1037/a0020907.

Duran, S., & Barlas, G. Ü. (2016). Effectiveness of psychoeducation intervention on subjective well being and self-compassion of individuals with mental disabilities. *International Journal of Research in Medical Sciences*, *4*(1), 181–188. http://dx.doi.org/10.18203/2320-6012.ijrms20160028.

Greenberg, J. L., Lewis, S. E., & Dodd, D. K. (1999). Overlapping addiction and self-esteem among college men and women. *Addictive Behaviors*, *24*(4), 565–571.

Kasali, R. (2014). *Disruption*. Jakarta: Gramedia.

Mcfarlane, W., Downing, D., & Dixon, L. (2012). Recent developments in family psychoeducation as an evidence-based practice. *Journal of Marital and Family Therapy*, *38*(1), 101–121. https://doi.org/10.1111/j.1752-0606.2011.00256.x.

Sage. (2019). Quasi-Experimental and single-case experimental design (pp. 333–370). Sage Publication, Inc.

Santrock, J. W. (2012). *Life-Span development* (13th ed.). McGraw Hill Social Sciences Language.

Sato, T. (2006). Internet addiction among students: Prevalence and psychological problems in Japan. *Japan Medical Association Journal*, *49*(7–8), 279–283.

Seniati, L., Yulianto, A., & Setiadi, B. (2011). *Psikologi Eksperimen*. Jakarta: PT. Indeks.

Sirisena, M. (2018). *Sri Lanka : In an era of global disruption, knowledge, technology are vital facts*. London.

Supratiknya, A. (2011). *Merancang program dan Modul Psikoedukasi*.

Torres-rodríguez, A., Griffiths, M. D., & Carbonell, X. (2018). The treatment of Internet Gaming Disorder : A brief overview of the PIPATIC Program, *International Journal of Mental Health & Addiction, 16, 1000–1015*. https://doi.org/10.1007/s11469-017-9825-0

Tripathi, A. (2017). Impact of Internet addiction on mental health : An integrative therapy is needed. *Integrative Medicine International*, *4*, 215–222. https://doi.org/10.1159/000491997.

Young, K., Pistner, M., O'Mara, J., & Buchanan, J. (2000). Cyber-Disorders: The mental health concern for the new millennium. *CyberPsychology & Behavior*, *5*(5), 475–479. https://doi.org/10.1089/cpb.1999.2.475.

Asti Meiza, Nani Nuranisah Djamal, and Ghina Sulthanah

Family Support for Adolescents in Drug Addiction Therapy

UIN Sunan Gunung Djati Bandung, Indonesia

Abstract: The increase in the number of drug addicts is one of the major problems in Indonesia. These addicts are found in various age groups, ranging from adults, teenagers, and even children. A person who is addicted to drugs would find it difficult to overcome the problem. The condition is called Craving and is the desire to return to using drugs. This research was conducted in Pamardi Putra Social Institution Galih Pakuan Bogor, one of the places for the rehabilitation of drug users. It aimed to determine whether Self-Efficacy (SE) and Social Support (SS) had an effect on Craving, either simultaneously or separately. The research design used was the correlational causality method, while the data collection technique was the questionnaire method, based on Bandura (1997) theory. The SS scale used was based on the theory of Sarafino and Smith (2011), while the Craving scale was based on Drummond theory (2001). Finally, the data was analyzed using the multiple linear regression method, and the subjects were 40 respondents. The results showed that SE and SS had various influences on the Craving of drug users. It also showed that the family plays a very important role as part of the SS for the success of the therapy process. However, the family referred to here constitutes of the closest people that accompany the subject during therapy at the rehabilitation center, and not father, mother, or siblings. Thus, they may be the officers and fellow friends who are already considered by the subject as family. It was also found that the content of Islamic values in therapeutic materials also gave positive qualities, which are contained in the therapy module book. Finally, the various activities prepared for the therapy were based on values and procedures in the Islamic religion.

Keywords: Self-efficacy, social support, craving, drugs addict

1 Introduction

Drug addicts of narcotics, psychotropics, and other addictive substances in Indonesia are found in various age groups ranging for adults to adolescents. Based on the application of the Narcotics Information System (SIN) belonging to the National Narcotics Agency or BNN, data obtained in the last five years (2012–2016) showed that there were 2,140 cases and the number increased every year (Ministry of Health, 2017).

Drugs affect the body, especially the brain/central nervous system, causing physical, psychological, and other social disorders (Anggreni, 2015). Every addict who wants to stop taking these substances would usually experience suggestions to re-use them, known as Craving (Clark, 2007). Another definition of craving is that it is the desire of addicts to reuse drugs after trying to stop the act (Fitriani, Subekti, & Aquarisnawati, 2011). Meanwhile, according to Fortuna and Smelson, 2008, in craving, there is a strong desire, which may be described as coercion or pressure, to reuse drugs, which makes it difficult for people to stop the act and, thus, backslide (Fortuna & Smelson, 2008). This condition is called Relapse (Kurniawan, Yuliawati, & Hamdani, 2017), and it occurs when a victim does not know how to divert or neutralize Cravings, and thus returns to the drug use behavior (Pranoto & Astuti, 2006). The majority of drug users have experienced Craving.

Factors that influence the emergence of craving (Pranoto & Astuti, 2006), include:

1. Internal factors that come from within a person namely self-awareness, and desire, and self-confidence (Self-Efficacy) to learn to build oneself and the intention and willingness to appreciate life.
2. External factors originating from the external environment, such as moving away from the environment that plunges a person into drug use, social support, friends, and attention from family and other people around.

2 Literature Review

The Ministry of Social Affairs of the Republic of Indonesia makes several special social and rehabilitation services to deal with victims of drug abuse. An example is the Pamardi Putra Social Institution Galih Pakuan in Bogor, which was established in 1983. As explained in the previous section, two factors that influence the emergence of Craving are Self-Efficacy (SE) and Social Support (SS) (Pranoto & Astuti, 2006).

The preliminary study showed that 7 out of 10 clients made their own beliefs that could help them regardless of drug abuse. This raises questions on why Craving and even Relapse still occur in those that have confidence in recovering from drug abuse.

Bandura (1997) defined SE as people's belief in their abilities in preparing and carrying out the actions needed to produce a specified achievement. Furthermore, according to Maddux, 2000, it is an individual's belief in one's skills that could be carried out in certain situations, and just not a skill (Maddux, 2000). In this case, self-efficacy is the beliefs and self-confidence of victims of drug abuse to avoid craving.

The research by Fitrianti, Subekti, and Aquarisnawati (2011) found a significant influence between emotional maturity and self-efficacy on the craving of former drug users. Meanwhile, other research found that family social support influenced the craving of such individuals (Maksum & Mabruri, 2016). The research proves that psychologically, appropriate social support would lead to feelings of appreciation, acceptance, attention, and love. This is the reason why one of the independent variables chosen is SS.

In this research, the SS was sourced from fellow clients and social care workers. This was based on the condition that the subjects more often met with friends at the sober living home officers, rather than with their own families.

SS is an effort to provide assistance to individuals to improve the quality of their mental health, confidence, enthusiasm or encouragement, and acceptance. This support can be sourced from people that are significant and have the same degree of involvement with the subject (Sarafino & Smith, 2011). Thus social support can be obtained from fellow drug addicts that are clients, and from the officers in the institution.

The therapeutic process is carried out in the form of a Therapeutic Community. In this type of therapy, clients help each other in addressing the problems they face. In other words, it involves people helping other persons, while also simultaneously receiving help from those persons. This is in line with Islamic values, as Allah says in the Qur'an in Surah Al Maidah verse 2 which means "And help in doing good and taqwa and do not help in sin and guilt. Also, be careful of Allah, surely Allah is severe in punishment." This is also confirmed by the Hadith narrated by Muttafaq'alaih, the Messenger of Allah which means "Whoever helps his brother's needs, Allah will help his needs." The assistance rendered to fellow citizens in rehabilitation homes for mutual strengthening in preventing craving would be an alarm that could remind them of the dangers of craving.

Community therapy is thought to reduce or eliminate craving in drug addicts. This therapy process is carried out gradually, by increasing the personal and social responsibilities of the addicts. The involvement of similar friends that live in rehabilitation places is a medium used by individuals to learn and assimilate social values, and develop more effective social skills in order that they could reduce or eliminate craving (Mullen & Faucette, 2011).

3 Method

This study used a quantitative approach with a causal research design. Furthermore, the technical data analysis was carried out using the multiple linear regression analysis (Sudjana, 2005), while the data collection technique was the questionnaire method.

3.1 Population/Sample

The subjects were 250 clients at the Pamardi Putra Social Institution Galih Pakuan Bogor, while the respondents were 40 of those clients. Besides, there are three stages that clients in the institution have to go through to be declared recovered from drug abuse, namely (1) New Add, (2) Induction, and (3) Primary Stage.

3.2 Measurement Tools

The scale used was the Likert scale. Also, the SE scale was the first independent variable and was based on dimensions according to Bandura (1997), namely, level, structure, and generality, with 28 items. This instrument had a reliability index of 0.95 as shown by the Cronbach's alpha test.

The SS scale was based on the dimensions according to Sarafino and Smith (2011), namely, emotional or esteem, tangible or instrumental, informational, and companion supports, with 33 items. Meanwhile, the Craving scale as the dependent variable was based on the dimensions according to Drummond (2001), which showed that craving would arise when victims of drug abuse receive visual, auditory, taste, smell, or touch stimuli associated with the drug they abuse, with 21 items.

As the reference, when the index is greater than 0.8, it shows that there is a very high validity. The SE scale validity test obtained index scores of 0.907, 0.959, and 0.874, respectively, for the three dimensions, namely, level, structure, and generality. Furthermore, the validity index scores for the SS scale consisting of four dimensions was 0.953 for the emotional or esteem support dimension, 0.806 for the tangible or instrumental support dimension, 0.814 for the informational support dimension, and 0.803 for the companionship dimension.

When the index score is between 0.61 and 0.8, it is said to have high validity. The Craving scale consisting of five dimensions, namely, visual, auditory, taste, olfactory, and palpable stimulus obtained index scores of 0.863, 0.830, 0.756, 0.752, and 0.780, respectively, for these dimensions.

The data analysis technique used to test the effect of SE and SS on the Craving of the clients was the multiple regression analysis. Furthermore, the tests used were the F-test and t-test. The F-test was conducted to determine the effect of all the independent variables simultaneously on the dependent variable, while the t-test was used to determine the effect of each independent variable individually on the dependent variable (Priyanto, 2012). Meanwhile, the formula used in the multiple regression analysis technique is shown as Equation (1):

$$\hat{Y} = ß_0 + ß_1 X_1 + ß_2 X_2 \quad (1)$$

$\hat{Y}$ = dependent variable (Craving)
$ß_0$ = constant
$ß_1, ß_2$ = Regression coefficient independent variable
X_1 = the first independent variable (SE)
X_2 = the second independent variable (SS)

4 Results

This study aims to determine whether or not the SE and SS variables influenced the Craving of the clients. However, unfortunately, this research did not obtain definite data on how long the respondents were treated.

4.1 Descriptive Analysis

Based on the descriptive results, the categories of the three variables can be seen in Figure 1.

The results showed that the SE of 2 clients (5%) were in a low category, while those of 32 clients (80%) were in the middle category, and 6 clients (15%), in the high category. This shows that SE were mostly in the middle category.

The SE of the clients were influenced by their self-experience and experienced by others. Furthermore, they were also influenced by a sense of calmness in facing the task, which was to escape from drug traps. According to Colondam, 2007, drug use causes a person to experience negative mental and behavioral changes. These experiences make it difficult for drug addicts to maintain their confidence to stop using drugs. However, the impacts of using drugs are not only expressed in mental and behavioral changes but also expressed in physiological changes. Finally, addictive substances consumed in the long term could reduce the function of nerves and organs.

Clients with SE in the high category had confidence and strength in releasing themselves from drug use. Therefore, they were not easily affected by the urge to re-use drugs. Meanwhile, clients with SE in the low category had low confidence

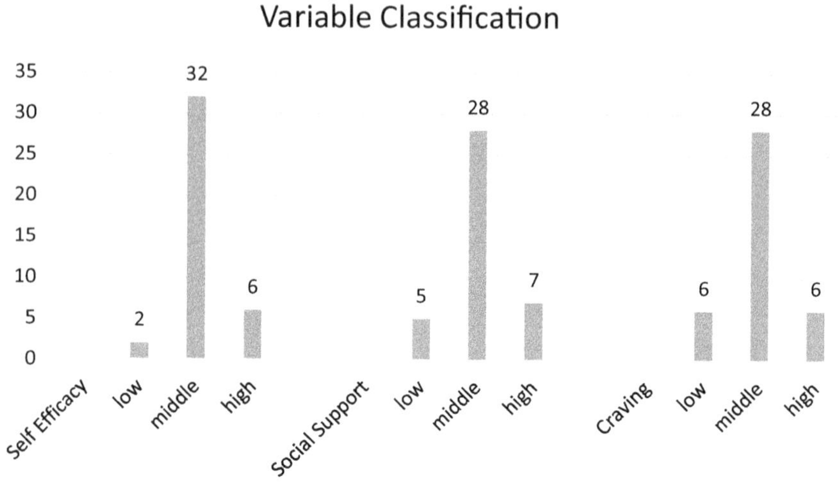

Figure 1. Categories of Variables Based on Mean and Standard Deviation

and strength in releasing themselves from drug use and, thus, experienced craving. The is very logical, considering that the role of self-efficacy in the recovery process of addicts (including craving) is very important. Individuals with low self-efficacy, who view life barriers as threats, focus more on their own shortcomings, and not on efforts to overcome problems. They also think that success would be difficult to achieve and that the results would be negative. The absence of a clear purpose in life, difficulty to commit to, give up quickly, and always attribute failure to their own personal deficiencies make individuals with low self-efficacy very vulnerable to stress, anxiety, and depression (Bandura, 1994).

Based on the preliminary study, data showed that 7 out of 10 clients who were rehabilitated at home had the desire to recover from drug use because of family support. Meanwhile, the obstacles in undergoing rehabilitation in a rehabilitation center make it difficult for clients to meet their families. Therefore, in this study, the role of the family as a source of social support was not shown to significantly affect craving.

There is a possibility that the role of the biological family would be replaced by the new family in rehabilitation centers. Therefore, the social support that clients get is more from community members in rehabilitation centers, rather than from their own biological family. According to the concept of community therapy, active participation in group life and activities could promote individual change and the achievement of therapeutic goals (Dye et al., 2009; Dye et al.,

2012; Vanderplasschen et al., 2013; Vanderplasschen et al., 2014; and Bunt et al., 2008). The emphasis is mainly on social learning and mutual assistance, where everyone in the rehabilitation center is responsible for the recovery of their peers. Assistance to others is seen as an important part of the process of changing oneself (De Leon, 2000; De Leon, 2015; and Sacks et al., 2012a).

The descriptive results for the craving showed that all clients were still experiencing craving even though they were in the final stage of the rehabilitation process. However, they had different levels of craving. The majority of the clients were in the middle category of craving. This means that although they were in the final stages of rehabilitation, there was still a chance that they would re-use drugs. For the ideal results to be obtained, clients are expected to not experience craving at all. Moreover, such a condition can be an indicator of the success of *the sober living home* in implementing rehabilitation programs.

As stated above, the craving of the majority of the clients was in the middle category. However, it is possible that this result was obtained because of the length of time the clients underwent rehabilitation. The results of a longitudinal study conducted by DATOS (Drug Abuse Treatment Outcome Studies) as quoted by Hubbard et al. (2003) showed that in community therapy, participants that showed an increase in behavior after one year would continue to do so after five years, provided the same modality of therapy is used. According to the National Institute of Health, 2015, the length of time for treatment is an important factor in community therapy. In this study, the length of time the subjects were in the rehabilitation center was not known with certainty. However, when the period is less than one year, there would be a low probability that SS would have an effect on the craving of the clients.

4.2 Inferential Analysis

4.2.1 Hypothesis Testing

The results in Table 1 showed that F=21,039 with a significance coefficient of 0,000 <0.05, meaning that H_0 was rejected. Therefore, SE and Social Support simultaneously influenced Craving. This implies that the SE and SS had an effect on the Craving of the clients.

Table 1. Regression Analysis Summary

	Unstandardized Coefficients		Standardized Coefficients			Collinearity Statistics	
Model	B	Std. Error	Beta	T	Sig.	Tolerance	VIF
1 (Constant)	81.167	8.456		9.599	.000		
X1	-.637	.099	-.800	-6.455	.000	.823	1.216
X2	.181	.084	.265	2.141	.039	.823	1.216

The t-test was used to determine the effect of the partial independent variables or each of the dependent variables. When the significance coefficient is smaller than the alpha value of 0.05, it means that there is a significant influence between each independent variable and the dependent variable.

Based on the results, the significance coefficient for the SE variable was 0.000, which is <0.05. This means that SE has a partial effect on Craving. Similarly, the significance coefficient for SS variable was 0.039, which was also <0.05. This means that SS had a partial effect on Craving. The influence of SE on Craving was -0.637.

4.2.2 Determination Coefficient (R^2)

The coefficient of determination functions to get a percentage of how influential the independent variables are on the dependent variable (Priyanto, 2013). Based on the results it was discovered that the determination coefficient value was 0.532, which means that 53.2% of Craving was influenced by the SE and SS variables, while the remaining 46.8% was influenced by other variables not examined in this research.

The regression equation model which aimed to ascertain whether SE and SS could affect craving in nursing clients obtained a significance level of 0.000. Furthermore, the results showed that the SE and SS variables had significance coefficients of 0.000 and 0.039, respectively. Based on these significance coefficient values, these variables have a partial effect on Craving. The regression model is shown in Equation (2):

$$\hat{Y} = 81.167 - 0.637X_1 + 0.181X_2 \quad (2)$$

The constant value (ß0) is 81.167, which means that when the SE and SS values are both 0, the level of Craving is positive at 81.167. Moreover, the SE (ß1) variable regression coefficient was -0.637, which is negative. This means that for every increase in SE by 1 unit, Craving would decrease by 0.637, assuming that another independent variable has a fixed value.

The regression coefficient value of the SS (ß2) variable was 0.181, which is positive. This means that when SS increases by 1 unit, Craving would increase by 0.181, assuming that another independent variable is fixed.

The F-test calculation obtained a significance coefficient of 0.000, which was <0.05. This means that H0 was rejected while H1 was accepted and that there were influences of SE and SS on the Craving of clients at the social home. The magnitude of the influence of SE and SS on Craving was 53.2%, while the remaining 46.8% was influenced by other variables not examined in this research.

In the classic test, multiple linear regression tests were also carried out in other tests, namely, Multicollinearity, Heteroscedasticity, and Autocorrelation Tests. The test results were carried out, and no disturbances were found in the regression model obtained. Therefore, the model was good to approach the problem of this research.

The results also showed that the SE and SS variables had a partial effect on Craving. Furthermore, the significance coefficient of the SE variable was 0.000, which was <0.05, while the SS variable had a significance coefficient value of 0.039, which was <0.05. Therefore, based on these answers, the Minor H_1 and H_2 hypothesis were accepted. The acceptance of H_1 means that there was an influence of SE on the Craving of the Drug Users, while the acceptance of H_2 means that SS has an effect on Craving.

The results showed that the SE (ß1) variable regression coefficient was -0.637, which was negative. This means that for every increase in SE of 1 unit, Craving would decrease by 0.637, assuming the value of another independent variable is fixed. Meanwhile, the SS (ß2) variable regression coefficient was 0.181, which was positive. This means that for every increase in SS of 1 unit, Craving would also increase by 0.181, assuming that another independent variable has a fixed value. This condition shows that SE could reduce the occurrence of Craving, unlike SS which cannot. This is because Craving occurs due to stimulus from the environment, and the SS also comes from external sources. Thus, the SS that the clients received provided a stimulus for them to experience craving.

Pamardi Putra Institution applies the Therapeutic Community (TC) program to reduce drugs craving. The target is the change of perception and the self-discovery that drives growth and change. The spirit of change in the intervention program is in line with the teachings of Islam. As mentioned by Al-Ajulani in Kasyful Khafa that the Prophet in his dream Abdul Aziz bin Abi Rawwad, which means "Whoever was two days (today and yesterday) the same then he has lost. Whoever is worse than the day before, he is a cursed one." (The person who is in the same condition today as yesterday is one of the losers. And if his condition today is worse than yesterday then he is a cursed person.)

5 Conclusion

The results of this study concluded that SE and SS had a simultaneous influence on the Craving of drug users in the Pamardi Putra Institution. However, craving is also influenced by other variables. One of the most important variables is the SS that comes from the family, which, in this condition, is the friends at the rehabilitation center.

SS, especially from families, was highly needed by clients during the therapy period. However, in reality, these clients were far from their families. The absence of information about how long the clients have been in the institution was one of the limitations of this study. This is because the period of therapy is one of the factors that contribute to the development of the SE and SS needed for success in suppressing the craving level of clients.

In the future, the therapy process could be changed by actively involving the real family to provide SS to the client. Furthermore, it is recommended that the contribution of Islamic values in the therapy process should be more optimized and that this contribution is one variable that could also be measured in subsequent studies.

6 Affiliations

1. Name: Asti Meiza
Institution: UIN Sunan Gunung Djati Bandung, Indonesia
Address: Jl.A.H.Nasution No.105, Cipadung, Cibiru, Bandung, Indonesia
E-mail: asti.meiza@uinsgd.ac.id

2. Name: Nani Nuranisah Djamal
Institution: UIN Sunan Gunung Djati Bandung, Indonesia
Address: Jl.A.H.Nasution No.105, Cipadung, Cibiru, Bandung, Indonesia
E-mail: nanindjamal@gmail.com

3. Name: Ghina Sulthanah
Institution: UIN Sunan Gunung Djati Bandung, Indonesia
Address: Jl.A.H.Nasution No.105, Cipadung, Cibiru, Bandung, Indonesia
E-mail: ghinasulthanah@gmail.com

7 References

Anggreni, D. (2015). Dampak bagi pengguna narkotika, psikotropika dan zat adiktif (napza) di kelurahan gunung kelua samarinda ulu. *E-Journal Sosiatri-Sosiologi, 3*(3), 37–51.

Bandura, A. (1997). *Self-Efficacy: The exercise of control.* New York: W. H. Freeman and Company.

Clark. (2007). *Menanggulangi NAPZA*. Bogor: Dana Bhakti Prima Yasa.

Colondam, Veronica. (2007). *Raising drug-free children*. Jakarta: Yayasan Cinta Anak Bangsa.

De Leon, George. (2000). *The therapeutic community*. Springer Publishing Company, Inc.

Drummond, D. C. (2001). Conceptualizing addiction: Theories of drug craving, ancient and modern. *Addiction, 96*, 33–46.

Fitriani, N., Subekti, E. A., & Aquarisnawati, P. (2011). Pengaruh antara Kematangan Emosi dan Self-eficacy terhadap Craving pada Mantan Pengguna Narkoba. *INSAN, 13*(02), 106–117.

Fortuna, J. L., & Smelson, D. A. (2008). The phenomenon of drug craving. *Journal of Psychoactive Drugs, 40*, 3.

Kementerian Sosial Republik Indonesia. (2017). *PSPP "Galih Pakuan" Bogor.* [Internet]. Diambil dari https://galihpakuan.kemsos.go.id/

Kesehatan, Kementerian. (2017). Anti Narkoba Sedunia. [Internet]. Diambil dari http://www.depkes.go.id/resources/download/pusdatin/infodatin/infodatin narkoba 2017.pdf

Kurniawan D., Yuliawati R., & Hamdani A. (2017). Hubungan antara keadaan keluarga dengan perilaku Relapse (kekambuhan) Narkoba pada residen. *Jurnal Kesehatan Masyarakat, 7*, 2.

Maddux, J. E. (2000). *Self-Efficacy: The power of believing you can. Handbook of positive psychology.* New York: Oxford University Press.

Maksum, & Mabruri. (2016). Pengaruh Dukungan Sosial Keluarga Terhadap Craving Pada Mantan Pengguna Narkoba. *Intuisi Jurnal Ilmiah Psikologi, 8*, 3.

Pranoto, L. S., & Astuti, Y. D. (2006). Pengaruh *Craving* dalam pencapaian kondisi *Clean and Sober* pecandu NAPZA. *Psikologika, 22*, XI.

Priyanto, D. (2012). *Cara Kilat Belajar analisis data dengan SPSS 20.*Yogyakarta: ANDI.

Purwanto, E. A., & Sulistyastuti, D. R. (2011), *Metode Penelitian Kuantitatif.* Yogyakarta: Gava Media.

Sarafino & Smith, E. P., & Smith, T. W. (2011). *Health psychology biopsychosocial interactions.* Edisi ketujuh. State of America: John Wiley & Sons Inc.

Sudjana. (2005). *Metode Statistika.* Bandung: Tarsito.

Therapeutic Communities (Reasearch Report Series), U.S Departement of Health and Human Services (National Institute of Health) NIH Publication Number 15-4877 • Revised July 2015. https://d14rmgtrwzf5a.cloudfront.net/sites/default/files/therapueticcomm_rrs_0723.pdf

Witrin Gamayanti, Ila Nurlaila Hidayat, Yasinta Sulun, and Endi

Self-Concept and Infidelity of Husbands Whose Wives Work Abroad as Women Workers

Universitas Islam Negeri Sunan Gunung Djati Bandung, Indonesia

Abstract. Working as a woman worker (Tenaga Kerja Wanita or TKW) has the consequences of separately living with the husband. One problem that often arises is infidelity by husbands on the grounds of meeting sexual needs. There is a belief among husbands whose wives are migrant workers that having an affair is a natural thing and it becomes an open secret among them and the surrounding community. This study aims to determine the relationship between self-concept and infidelity of husbands whose wives work as TKW. This research uses correlational quantitative method with simple linear regression analysis. The subjects are 33 husbands whose wives work as TKW coming from one of the villages in Kabupaten Indramayu (Indramayu Regency). The instrument used in this research consists of a self-concept scale and an infidelity scale. The results show that there is no significant relationship between self-concept and the husband's infidelity.

Keywords: Self-concept, infidelity, woman worker

1 Introduction

Until 2018, West Java was in the top rank as the supply province of Indonesian migrant workers, in which Kabupaten Indramayu (Indramayu Regency) was ranked first in the region that supplied the most Indonesian migrant workers (Tampomuri, 2019; Mualim, 2018). In terms of social and cultural factors, Kinanthi, Ginanjar, and Wilman (2018) say the Indramayu people have a consumptive lifestyle, have a habit of being in debt, want to get rich quickly, and do not want to lose materially to compete with others.

Based on interviews with a number of research subjects and community leaders, the goal of women becoming TKW is to make their economic life better, but in reality, the money sent every month to the family is partly used by the husband to commit infidelity with the aim of channeling sexual needs because his wife has long left him.

Infidelity is also defined as adultery, cheating, or unfaithfulness (Rokach & Philibert-Lignières, 2015). Fife, Weeks, and Gambescia (2008, in Schonian,

2013) state infidelity as a betrayal of commitments regarding sexual and emotional intimacy either implicitly or openly. Infidelity shares emotional and/or sexual intimacy with another person without the consent of the partner. Whereas Luo, Cartun, and Snider (2010, in Martins, Pereira, Andrade, Dattilio, Narciso, & Canavarro, 2016) suggest the term "extradyadic involvement" which means involvement in sexual and/or emotional relationships with people other than the primary partner, which is carried out in exclusive romance relationships.

Infidelity can occur in women and men with motivational reasons related to dissatisfaction with relationships and both seeking emotional and sexual behavior (Scheeren, de Apellániz, & Wagner, 2018). Other causes are gaps in sexual life with the partner (Yeniçeri & Kkdemir, 2006); seeking sexual gratification (Palencia, Rivera-Aragón, & Díaz-Loving, 2007); drive, innate and male instincts (Goldenberg, 2011); and curiosity and pleasure as well as variation of sexual partners (Scheeren et al., 2018). This is also experienced by husbands whose wives become TKW. Based on the results of interviews with the research subjects, it is known that what causes the infidelity is the sexual needs of the husbands that are not fulfilled. There is a belief in them that having an affair is better than remarrying because of the consequences that they will be sued for divorce by the wives who finance their life so far.

The reasons of infidelity committed by a husband whose wife becomes a TKW is very contrary to the religious, moral, cultural, and social norms that exist in Indonesia in general. Researchers see there are certain things that underlie the decision-making, so they have an affair. One of the things that underlie the quality of a person's behavior is self-concept. Self-concept is a central theme on which most aspects of personality are regulated. The importance of self-concept lies in its influence on the quality of one's behavior and its adaptation to life and various situations at hand (Dhingra, Sharma, & Kour, 2017). The affair of husbands whose wives working as TKW in Kedungwungu Village, Indramayu Regency, is not a strange thing; it seems understandable, so it becomes an open secret. Researchers suspect there is a possibility that the affair is related to the self-concept that they form based on their understanding of community assessment of husbands who are left by their wives who work as TKW.

Bracken (2009) distinguishes between positive and negative self-concepts. In this study, if the husband's self-concept is positive, then he will become the husband who is responsible for his marriage by not committing infidelity. Meanwhile, if the husband's self-concept is negative, then he will become a husband who is less responsible for his marriage so that when his sexual needs are not met, he will commit infidelity. Based on this, the researchers want to know the correlation between the husband's self-concept and infidelity.

2 Literature Review

Fitts (1971) says that self-concept is self – as seen, felt, and experienced by oneself. He also reveals that the self-concept is the most prominent aspect that affects human behavior and is a concept that can explain variables and influence human behavior such as motives, needs, attitudes, values, and personality. Another definition of self-concept is a collection of knowledge, ideas, attitudes, and beliefs about what is in oneself (Krause, Bochner, & Duchesne, 2006). There are many theories about self-concept, and they agree that the concept of self is not owned by people from birth but exists along with the development of one's understanding (Fitts, 1971). Individuals acquire self-concept as a function of their direct and indirect interaction with environmental factors. In particular, people receive positive or negative feedback about their behavior or attributes from two feedback modes or perspectives, namely directly from their personal experiences (personal perspective) and indirectly from other individuals in their environment (other perspectives) (Bracken, 2009).

According to Fitts and Warren (1996, in Fin & Ishak, 2014), the non-academic self-concept consists of five aspects, namely, social, physical, moral and ethical, personal, and family aspects. The physical self-concept is a person's view of health, appearance, physical skills, and sexuality. Moral and ethical self-concepts measure the extent to which a person is satisfied with their own behavior, which is related to feelings of being able to control their own impulses and behavior. The personal self-concept provides input to a person's sense of self-sufficiency and self-determination regardless of physical attributes or relationships with others. The self-concept of the family reflects how people view themselves in relation to their family and close associates. The social self-concept provides an indication of how individuals perceive themselves in relation to peers, in addition to family members and close friends.

Infidelity is an act of violating the partner's trust that is beyond the limit and involves a special agreement with another person (cheating partner) without the knowledge of the primary partner (Schonian, 2013). This action is carried out with the intention of building an intimate relationship with another person that causes emotional pain to the primary partner. There are three dimensions of infidelity (Schonian, 2013), namely: physical infidelity, emotional infidelity, and online infidelity (cyber infidelity). Whitty and Quigley (2008) say that online infidelity is as high as sexual infidelity. Factors that affect infidelity can be personal factors, factors related to husband–wife relationships, and factors related to the context or environment (Scheeren et al., 2018).

3 Method

This research uses correlational quantitative method, aims to test the independent variable, namely, self-concept with the dependent variable, namely, husband's infidelity. Data analysis uses simple linear regression analysis. The population consists of 33 husbands who have wives working as TKW, residing in the village of Kedungwungu, Kabupaten Indramayu, aged between 20 and 50 years, with the length of marriage between 1 and 25 years.

Data collection uses Likert scale. The self-concept scale is made based on the theory of Fitts and Warren (1996, in Fin & Isaac, 2014). Of the 76 items, there are 25 items that meet the requirements. The validity calculation uses the Pearson Product Moment correlation test, and it obtained a value of. 377–.922 indicating that the level of validity is moderate and very high, although there is one dimension that is classified as low, namely physical self. The reliability test result shows a value of. 945 which means that the self-concept scale is classified as reliable. The scale of infidelity is based on the concept of Schonian (2013). Of the 32 items, there are 25 items that meet the requirements. The validity test results of. 786 and. 965 indicate that the two dimensions have a high level and a very high level of validity, which means that this measuring instrument is valid. This scale is also classified as reliable with a value of. 922.

4 Results

The results of the classical assumption test show that the data are normally distributed (sig. 115>. 05) and linearly related (sig. 967>. 05). The results of the F test in Table 1 show a significance value of. 392>. 05. Therefore, it can be concluded that there is no significant relationship between self-concept and husband's infidelity. In further calculations, it is obtained that the value of R square is.024, so the role of self-concept on husband's infidelity is 2.4% and 97.6% related to other factors.

Table 1. The Results of the F Test

Model	Sum of Squares	df	Mean Square	F	Sig.
Regression	87.413	1	87.413	.755	.392[a]
Residual	3590.619	31	115.826		
Total	3678.032	32			

The results show that there is no significant relationship between self-concept and the husband's infidelity. They have a positive self-image, namely believing that as husbands they are good husbands, loyal and reliable to their wives, and feel satisfied with themselves. Fitts (1971) states that self-concept is a person's way of seeing self-images, beliefs, judgments including physical, emotional, intellectual, and spiritual based on what he understands from his environment and influences a person's interaction with that environment. In this study, the environmental context in question is the environmental conditions of the community where the subjects live.

Researchers assume that the rejection of the hypothesis can be due to several things, namely: first, the level of education, Fitts (1971) says that the level of education affects a person's self-concept. In this case, it is known that the educational background of the respondents are 12 elementary school graduates, 12 junior high school graduates, and 9 high school graduates. So there may be mistakes in managing the concept of "right and wrong" or "good and bad" so that when the environment around has values that are contrary to religious and moral values, the ability to digest and sort information is less developed. Second, the cultural and value factors that develop in the community where the respondents live, namely, people want prosperity without working hard, adhere to a culture of wealth competition, and perceive that it is easier for women to find work and can meet family needs. Further, they are prouder when they have daughters because their daughters are considered to increase the family status. The belief that a husband whose wife works abroad may commit infidelity is a normal thing. It is normal to fulfill their sexual needs, and having an affair is better than remarriage.

The condition of the community, which has long been the biggest pocket of TKW in Indonesia, is gradually changing the paradigm of husband's self-concept and infidelity. The values that develop in the community are what researchers suspect make the husband's self-concept remain positive, even though as a husband he relies on his wife to improve the family economy and has an affair using money sent by his wife.

5 Conclusion

This study shows there is no significant relationship between self-concept and husband's infidelity, considering that its contribution is only 2.4%. The reason why the husbands have a positive self-concept is because the husbands have high personal self-values, so they believe that they are good husbands they want to be, husbands that wives can rely on, feel satisfied with who they are, and feel that they are loyal husbands, where loyalty is interpreted as the opportunity to commit infidelity as long as he does not marry again.

6 Affiliations

1. Name: Witrin Gamayanti
Institution: Universitas Islam Negeri Sunan Gunung Djati Bandung
Address: Jalan A.H. Nasution Nomor 105 Cibiru Bandung 40614
E-mail: witrin.gamayanti@uinsgd.ac.id

2. Name: Ila Nurlaila Hidayat
Institution: Universitas Islam Negeri Sunan Gunung Djati Bandung
Address: Jalan A.H. Nasution Nomor 105 Cibiru Bandung 40614
E-mail: ila.nurlaila@uinsgd.ac.id

3. Name: Yasinta Sulun
Institution: Universitas Islam Negeri Sunan Gunung Djati Bandung
Address: Jalan A.H. Nasution Nomor 105 Cibiru Bandung 40614
E-mail: yashenta@gmail.com

4. Name: Endi
Institution: Universitas Islam Negeri Sunan Gunung Djati Bandung
Address: Jalan A.H. Nasution Nomor 105 Cibiru Bandung 40614
E-mail: endi@uinsgd.ac.id

7 References

Bracken, B. A. (2009). Positive self-concepts. In M. J. Huebner, E. S., Gwang-soo, K., & Furlong. (Ed.), *Handbook of positive psychology in schools* (pp. 89–106). Taylor & Francis.

Dhingra, R., Sharma, N., & Kour, G. (2017). Assessment of self concept among Anganwadi workers of ICDS project, R.S Pura block of Jammu district. *International Research Journal of Human Resources and Social Sciences*, *4*(10), 162–172.

Fin, L. S., & Ishak, Z. (2014). Non-academic self concept and academic achievement: The indirect effect mediated by academic self concept. *Research Journal in Organizational Psychology & Educational Studies*, *3*(3), 184–188.

Fitts, W. H. (1971). *Self concept and self actualization*. Western Psychological Services Publishers and Distributor.

Goldenberg, M. (2011). *Por que homens e mulheres traem?* BestBolso.

Kinanthi, M. R., Ginanjar, A., & Wilman, W. (2018). Faktor-faktor bioekologi pada komitmen pernikahan tenaga kerja wanita asal Indramayu. *JPIB: Jurnal Psikologi Islam Dan Budaya*, *1*(2), 113–130. https://doi.org/10.15575/jpib.v1i2.2932

Krause, K. L., Bochner, S., & Duchesne, S. (2006). *Educational psychology for learning and teaching second edition*. Cengage Learning Australia.

Martins, A., Pereira, M., Andrade, R., Dattilio, F. M., Narciso, I., & Canavarro, M. C. (2016). Infidelity in dating relationships: Gender-specific correlates of face-to-face and online extradyadic involvement. *Archives of Sexual Behavior*, *45*(1), 193–205. https://doi.org/10.1007/s10508-015-0576-3

Mualim, I. (2018). *Daerah ini paling banyak kirim TKI*. Warta Ekonomi. https://www.wartaekonomi.co.id/read190583/daerah-ini-paling-banyak-kirim-tki

Palencia, A. R., Rivera-Aragón, S., & Díaz-Loving, R. (2007). Desarrollo del inventario multidimensional de infidelidad (IMIN). *Revista Iberoamericana de Diagnóstico Y Evaluación Psicológíca*, *23*(1), 121–147.

Rokach, A., & Philibert-Lignières, G. (2015). Intimacy, loneliness & infidelity. *The Open Psychology Journal*, *8*(Suppl 2-M3), 71–77.

Scheeren, P., de Apellániz, I. dA. M., & Wagner, A. (2018). Marital infidelity: The experience of men and women. *Trends in Psychology*, *26*(1).

Schonian, S. (2013). *Perception and definition of infidelity: A multimethod study*. University of Nevada Lasvegas.

Tampomuri, H. R. (2019). *Tiga propinsi jawa dan NTB jadi pemasok TKI terbesar*. Indonesia Global Worker News. https://indonesiaglobalworker.com/2019/07/05/tiga-provinsi-jawa-dan-ntb-jadi-pemasok-tki-terbesar-2/

Whitty, M. T., & Quigley, L. (2008). Emotional and sexual infidelity offline and in cyberspace. *Journal of Marital and Family Therapy*, *34*(4), 461–468.

Yeniçeri, Z., & Kkdemir, D. (2006). University students' perceptions of, and explanations for, infidelity: The development of the infidelity questionnaire (INFQ). *Social Behavior and Personality*, *34*(6), 639–650.

Sarbini, Moh. Dulkiah and Dr. Endi, MA.

Social Control of Blocking Radicalism Community in Reducing Juvenile Delinquency

Universitas Islam Negeri Sunan Gunung Djati Bandung, Indonesia

Abstract: This study aims to examine the social control of the Blocking Radicalism Community (BRC) in reducing juvenile delinquency. Researchers applied a qualitative approach by extracting data from observation and in-depth interviews. The participants are adolescents living in Cipadung Urban Village, Ujung Berung District, Bandung City, West Java, Indonesia. Using Travis Hirschi's theory of social control that assumes that deviation is a result of lack of control or social control, this study finds the following results. First, social control by BRC in handling deviant behaviors was carried out informally in the form of reprimand, advice, and information dissemination. Second, BRC develops an attachment model that is carried out through a heart-to-heart approach in the form of self-awareness to encourage a better behavior. Juveniles are encouraged to participate in various activities, such as social activities; activities related to hobbies, interests, and talents; and recreation and creative activities. Third, the Blocking Radicalism Community seeks to emphasize trust by nurturing moral values of the juveniles. Overall, this study concludes that social control of the Blocking Radicalism Community has an important role in reducing juvenile delinquency in urban areas.

Keywords: Juvenile delinquency, social control, deviant

1 Introduction

Juvenile delinquency is a deviant behavior carried out by adolescents. This behavior is usually synonymous with negative things that are usually done by young children and usually with their peers (Rathinabalan, 2017). Generally, this deviant behavior is referred to all actions, both individuals and groups, that deviate and even conflict with social values and norms, as well as the existed culture in society. This behavior occurs because someone ignores the norm or does not comply with the standards in society (Mojares et al., 2015).

This deviant behavior always occurs in society. Deviant behavior is not a person's personal quality. Since it occurs because of the values, norms, and culture that exists in society, this behavior can have positive or negative consequences in community life. Deviant behavior is the only behavior that is not in harmony with the guidelines of values, norms, and culture that regulates our life in society (Mohideen et al., 2016).

Sociologically, juvenile delinquency is a pathology caused by social neglect causing adolescents to develop deviant forms of behavior. Delinquency is related to the relationship between parents and legacy (Costello et al., 2020). Social and cultural environment have a great influence in contributing to the development of deviant behaviors in adolescents. This form of deviant behaviors shows that there is no adjustment to social norms in society.

Crime is anything that violates the law/crime, and often it occurs in big cities involving teenagers. Juvenile delinquency has now led to criminal acts, such as stealing, brawls, killing, striking, and even raping (Gunarsa & Singgih, 2003). The two common causes of adolescent deviations are internal factors or factors from within (self-control of teenagers) and external factors (social environment, family, and peers). Another factor is the lack of supervision from institutions or police to deal with and follow up on adolescents who commit to criminal acts. At present, juvenile delinquency has shifted to crime. Someone can commit to criminal acts because of the pressure to provide life necessities. Many crimes committed by groups involve teenagers (Sharma, et al., 2009).

The following data, from the Central Statistics Agency/Badan Pusat Statistik (BPS), Indonesia, shows an increase in juvenile delinquency within a span of years. In 2013, the number of juvenile delinquency in Indonesia reached 6,325 cases, while in 2014 the number reached 7,007 cases, and in 2015, reached 7,762 cases. It can be concluded that, from 2013 to 2014, the cases increased by 10.7%. Furthermore, the number of juvenile delinquency in Indonesia reached 8,597 cases in 2016 and 9,523 cases in 2017. Among these numbers are various cases of juvenile delinquency, including kidnapping, murder, free sex, and drug abuse.

2 Literature Review

This research uses Travis Hirschi's Social Control Theory (1969). This theory states that deviation is the result of a vacuum of control or social control (Narwoko & Suyanto, 2007). Social control theory has been tested and is still being cited (Ford, 2017; Van Glad, 2018). According to Hirschi, the key to high self-control learning is information dissemination, especially during someone's childhood. Parents can help their children to develop self-control by watching them and punishing their deviant actions (Henslin, 2006). The assumption of the theory is that every human being tends to be disobedient to the law or has an urge to violate the law. This theory assesses deviant behavior as a logical consequence of one's failure to obey the law, parallel with the theory of conformity (Fatkhuri, 2016).

Hirschi develops control theory into several theoretical propositions (Narwoko & Suyanto, 2007). First, various forms of denying social rules are the result of failure to socialize individual citizens to act in conformity with the existing rules. Second, irregularities and even crime or criminal behavior are evidences of the failure of conventional social groups, such as families, schools, or educational institutions and other dominant groups, to bind individuals to conform. Third, internal controls are more influential than external controls.

The stronger the individual's relationship with the community, the more effective the individual's inner control. Relationship is based on ties: (1) attachment (perceived affection and respect for people who conform to community norms); (2) commitment (having a solid part in a society, such as a respectable position in the family, a good dignity in college, a good job); (3) involvement (donating time and energy into agreed activities); and (4) belief (believe that certain actions are morally wrong) (Henslin, 2006).

Juvenile delinquency is also studied in the theory of social control by Travis Hirchi. According to Hirschi, social control is a concept that refers to distrust of someone leading them to have a tendency to violate norms in society. One of the common causes of deviant behavior in adolescents is internal social control, which is reasonable during the childhood period towards adolescence. During this period, social control is often inexistent, and there is no social norm. At this point, Hirschi agreed with Durkheim that one's behavior reflects a variety of their views on good customs, courtesy, and civilization (Maliki & Zainuddin, 2012).

One of the factors that influences adolescents to engage in delinquent acts is socioeconomic condition. This refers to Hirschi's theory in which he explains that juvenile delinquency deviation occurs because internal control is more influential than external control. Internal control includes family. Hirschi stated that the role of the family during adolescence period is crucial to form good behaviors or manners in adolescents.

Juvenile delinquency committed by adolescents is a social problem that has been a societal concern. The mischievous acts committed by teenagers to date are almost countless. In addition, they will not stop doing naughty shows until they receive the consequences. As a result of juvenile delinquency, people in their environment become negatively affected, which hurts the environment.

Delinquent acts committed by adolescents often generate anxiety and unpleasant feelings for their environment, specifically their parents. The only group of people who will have pleasant feelings from their acts are their peers because they are all equally in the search for identity. These delinquent acts that cause environmental resentment are often called juvenile delinquency (Sumara et al., 2017). By definition, juvenile delinquency is an evil behavior (*dursila*) or crime/ delinquency of young children. It is a symptom of social pain (pathology) in children and adolescents because of social negligence, triggering them to develop deviant forms of behavior (Kartono, 2017).

3 Research Method

This research applied a qualitative approach (Gordis, 2014), By definition, research methodology is also called research procedures, including determining research methodology, type of data to be collected, source of data to be extracted, how to collect data, and how to process and analyze data. This research has taken place in Cipadung Ujungberung Urban Village, Bandung City. Researchers implemented a field research to collect primary data from participants, conducted observations and interviews, and searched for additional documents needed in this study. There were 10 teenagers consisting of 5 girls and 5 boys as participants in this study. They are all adolescents who live and do activities in Cipadung and have committed delinquent acts. In addition, researchers also interviewed five youth organizers who are active in preventing juvenile delinquency. The data sources referenced in this study are divided into two, namely: primary data and secondary data sources. The primary data are village youth who have committed to delinquency acts. Meanwhile, secondary data are from documents and books to obtain and explore basic theories of experts related to the problems being studied. The interview guidelines involved three questions. First, how do adolescents commit juvenile crimes and act radically? Second, how do youth leaders exercise social control over adolescents who commit delinquency and radical acts? Third, how are the actions taken for adolescents who commit delinquency and radical acts? Furthermore, this study used several data collection techniques, such as library research as well as observation and interview techniques for empirical research.

4 Result

Based on some findings in the field, juvenile delinquency that is used to be committed include fighting, riding a motorbike without a driving license, being free, using drugs, and skipping school. The forms of juvenile delinquency that occur in Cipadung Village are very diverse. We categorize them into three categories of juvenile delinquency. First, delinquency acts that cause physical casualties to other people, in this case, include fighting and drinking because they can hurt others under the influence of alcohol. Second, social mischief that does not cause casualties on others, in this case, include drug abuse, free sex, or dating. Third, delinquency acts against status, in this case, include consuming liquor, smoking, participating in motorcycle gangs, and watching porn videos. Factors that influence the occurrence of juvenile delinquency in Cipadung Village are both factors from within and outside the adolescents. Factors from within that contribute to juvenile delinquency include low self-control and social perception, inability to adjust to good and creative environmental changes, and inexistent of healthy hobbies. Meanwhile, factors from outside include lack of attention and supervision from parents, lack of means of channeling leisure time, influence of technological developments, and improper peer influence. Blocking Radicalism Community provides an important role in reducing and preventing juvenile delinquency.

The Community tackles juvenile delinquency through preventive and curative efforts targeting adolescents who have committed to delinquency acts and prevent those who have not. Preventive actions are carried out by this Community through (1) juvenile delinquency counseling; (2) seminars; and (3) books (from an early age to promote good behaviors). Meanwhile, curative actions or restoring the situation are carried out by this Community through two activities. The first is training activities supporting interests and talents of the adolescents, such as Photography Training and Literary Training (Poetry Writing, Poetry Reading, and Storytelling). The second is routine activities, such as Book Club every Saturday and Sunday, Park Read Road to School, and Jamming Sessions in which everyone is required to pay with a book once a month. These two activities succeeded in reducing the number of juvenile delinquency in Cipadung Village. They play an active role in establishing a social control dealing with teenagers' problems through a creative approach and adjustment to the current trend.

Researchers believe that the social control established by the Community in directing deviant behaviors towards good behaviors is quite effective. Efforts put by the Blocking Radicalism Community, among others, are carried out through activities that are held regularly. Attachment or affection created by the Community restores the behavior of adolescents who experience irregularities. Most teenagers in the city are more concerned with having fun and hanging out with their peers that more often than not bring them to commit to delinquent acts. This attachment continues to be built through a heart-to-heart approach that tries to create awareness among adolescents to opt for a positive life. After attachment is built, commitment is carried out through an approach called the rule of binding or obeying the rules. The Community gives insights to the adolescents and works to build their mindsets through routine meetings or discussions, sometimes over a cup of coffee. After forming a family, the adolescents then have two choices. First, they will receive an appreciation or benefits, such as a bright future, if they decide to continue to be involved in positive activities. Second, they will receive a punishment, such as being outcasted or imprisoned, if they repeat their deviant behaviors. The relationship between attachment and commitment cannot be separated from social control in society. If the process of forming both goes well, the smaller is the level of deviation. In this case, the process of social control carried out by the Blocking Radicalism Community goes well that it can reduce the level of juvenile delinquency.

Involvement by the Community is implemented through positive activities involving teenagers. The Community tries to adjust the lifestyles of the adolescents in Cipadung Village with a hope that they will start leaving negative things. These activities are in the form of social activities, trainings to support hobbies, recreation, creative activities, and routine activities, including opening a library for free every Saturday and Sunday and conducting information dissemination on drug prevention and free sex.

The Blocking Radicalism Community designs activities with an objective to reduce the amount of delinquency acts. Adolescents are encouraged to fill in their leisure time by participating in a forum to talk about their hobbies, interests, and talents. In addition, in order to prevent adolescents who have not committed delinquency acts, the Community instills a reading culture from an early age with a hope that young children have an understanding and insight of which things are positive and which are negative.

Believe (trust) is also nurtured by the Community with a hope that the adolescents obey the rules and norms applied in society. Through these efforts of information dissemination and activities of reading from an early age, the adolescents are gradually aware. They begin to obey the rules and do not violate the norms.

These two approaches, Involvement and Believe, have a strong impact on the lives of the adolescents fostered by the Community. Efforts and activities conducted encourage the adolescents to be more creative in spending their leisure time as well as raise their awareness on obeying the rules and norms.

5 Conclusion

Social control conducted by Blocking Radicalism Community is relevant in changing the mindset and pattern of attitudes of adolescents, preventing them from committing delinquency acts. In other words, delinquency acts committed by adolescents can be reduced through informal social control, in the form of warning, advice, and encouragement, as the Community does. The community-developed model takes an attachment form that is carried out through a heart-to-heart approach to build awareness of good behavior. Some forms of activities that can bind adolescents include social activities, hobby-based activities, talent-and-interest-based activities, and recreation and creativity. The Community also seeks to emphasize the aspect of adolescent self-confidence in the form of moral nurturing to change to a better direction. In conclusion, community groups have an important role in reducing juvenile delinquency.

6 Affiliations

1. Name: Sarbini
Institution: UIN Sunan Gunung Djati Bandung
Address: Jln. A.H. Nasution No 105 Kota Bandung
E-mail: sarbini1@uinsgd.ac.id

2. Name: Moh. Dulkiah
Institution: UIN Sunan Gunung Djati Bandung
Address: Jln. A.H. Nasution No 105 Kota Bandung
E-mail: moh.dulkiah@uinsgd.ac.id

3. Name: Dr. Endi M.A
Institution: UIN Sunan Gunung Djati Bandung
Address: Jln. A.H. Nasution No 105 Kota Bandung
E-mail: endi@uinsgd.ac.id

7 References

Costello, Barbara J., & John H. Laub. (2020). Social control theory: The legacy of Travis Hirshi's causes of delinquency. *The Annual Review of Criminology*. Online atcrimino; annualreviews. Doi.org/10.1146/annualreviews.Doi.org/10.11419-041527.

Ford, T. L. (2017). Life unfiltered: Social control theory in the age of social media and substance abuse. PhD Diss., SamHouston State Univ., Hunsville, TX.

Glad, Van. (2018). Social control, family structure, and juvenile delinquency in fragile families. PhD Diss., Suny, Albany, NY.

Gordis, L. (2014). Case-control and other study designs. In: *Epidemiology* (5th ed., pp. 189–214). Philadelphia: Elsevier/Saunders.

Gunarsa, Ny. Singgih D. (2003). *Psikologi Remaja*. Jakarta: Gunung Mulia.

Henslin, James M. (2006). *Sosiologi Dengan Pendekatan Membumi*. Jakarta: Erlangga.

Kartono, Kartini. (2017). *Patologi Sosial 2 Kenakalan Remaja*. Jakarta: Rajawali Pers.

Maliki, Zainuddin. (2012). *Rekontruksi Teori Sosial Modern*. Yogyakarta: Gadjah Mada University Press.

Mohideen, R. S., Anuar, N. K. K., Latiff, D. I. A., Ridzuan, A. R., Kamarudin, F. H. (2016). Social factors that contribute juvenile delinquency at Melaka. *International Journal of Social Sciences and Education,* (3), 93–98.

Mojares, R. E., Evangelista, C. J. R., Escalona, R. A., & Ilagan, K. J. (2015). Impact of social networking to juvenile delinquency. *International Journal of Management Sciences, 5*(8): 582–586.

Narwoko, J. Dwi, & Suyanto, Bagong. (2007). *Sosiologi: Teks Pengantar & Terapan*. Jakarta: Kencana.

Rathinabalan, I., & Naaraayan, S. A. (2017). Effect of family factors on juvenile delinquency. *International Journal of Contemporary Pediatrics, 4*(6), 2079–2082.

Sharma, B. R., Dhillon, S., & Bano, S. (2009). Juvenile delinquency in India: A cause for concern. *Journal of Indian Academy of Forensic Medicine, 31*(1), 68–72.

Sumara, D. S., Humaedi, S., & Santoso, M. B. (2017). Kenakalan remaja dan penanganannya. Prosiding Penelitian Dan Pengabdian Kepada Masyarakat, 4(2), 129-389.

Syahrial Syarbiani, Fatkhuri. (2016). *Teori Sosiologi Suatu Pengantar*. Bogor: Ghalia Indonesia.

Indri Utami Sumaryanti and Fanni Putri Diantina

The Live Experiences of Fathers (The New Concept of a Father)

Universitas Islam Bandung, Indonesia

Abstract. Employing an adapted Interpretive Phenomenological Analysis (IPA) method, the experience of prominent figures as a father are explored. This chapter explores these two prominent figures' upbringing process in determining their parenting philosophy and their fatherhood practice. The two prominent figures are successful community leaders and heads of the university, engaged in a hermeneutic discussion regarding their experience as a father. Exploration of the data gathered from this discussion using the adapted IPA methodology evidenced two subordinate themes: (1) establishing fathering philosophy and (2) implementing fathering ways; included five emergent themes, namely: (1) compromising their parents' past parenting, (2) religious point of view, (3) I am able, (4) making the impossible possible, and (5)Wife supports. These themes are discussed in the context of contemporary literature by exploring the experiences of father roles. The subject interviewed in this study were questioned: "how was the upbringing process experienced" and "how did they determine and implement their parenting philosophy?"

Keywords: Interpretative phenomenologycal analysis, father figure, fatherhood

1 Introduction

The birth of the new concept of Father (Lamb, 1986), both provider and co-parent in all child-rearing activities, challenge every father. Robin, Dyer, Mc Bride, (2019) father role was a new emphasis on equal parenting that jump-started the scholarly study of father involvement. Today fathers are expected to be more active caregivers. However, since the 1997 IMF financial crisis, because of changes in the patriarchal family culture and the gender role differentiation within families (Kim & Lee, 2014), fathers and mothers are expected to be equal co-parents. Children's problems are no longer the mother's sole responsibility; instead, they are a common issue for both parents to attend to and deal with together (Hwang & Hwang, 2014).

Recently, as young fathers' involvement in child-rearing has increased, fathers spend more time with their children and show an increased interest in quality interactions, which can provide stability to their relationships with their children (Jo & Park, 2017). On the contrary Chen (2002) found that about 90% of fathers spent less than one hour each day with their children. Chen also identified two main reasons for fathers' low involvement in childcare: fathers' busy work conditions not leaving them enough time for involvement, and their beliefs that childcare belongs to women.

To understand fathering, Lamb (2010) recommends examining the father's role related to community expectations and cultural aspirations as well as comparing the roles of fathers in different countries. In Baldwin, Faulkner, Hecht, and Lindsley (2006), the father's roles have been transformed in many countries. Cultures determine people's fathering views (Gonzalez-Mena, 2008; Izumi-Taylor, Lee, & Franceschini, 2011) and influence their values, beliefs, and attitudes (Fagan & Palm, 2004; Ito & Izumi-Taylor, 2013).

Research on fathering indicates that the culture of fathering and the conduct of fathers have influenced societal and political changes (Fagan & Palm, 2004; La Rossa, 1997). In Japan, for instance, based on societal needs, the government has been supporting father involvement by promoting legislation for paternity leave since 2005 (Cabinet Office of Japan, 2009). Also, the Ministry of Health, Labour and Welfare of Japan (2011) launched a new program to support fathers, enabling them to balance work and child-rearing.

This study aims to understand better the fathers' involvement in children's upbringing. This study also considers several factors that may influence the father's involvement, such as the roles in their jobs or communities and the lack of policy that supports the work and childcare balance.

2 Literature Review

The Bioecological Model emphasized by Cabrera et al. (2014) states that fathers play an active and dynamic role that accounts for reciprocal relationships among the central aspects of the Bioecological Model: process, person, context, and time. From a bioecological perspective, development occurs during direct, ongoing, reciprocal, and increasingly complex proximal processes—the "process" aspect of the model—which, in the present case, would include fathers' regular and direct involvement with their children.

However, the processes' effect is moderated by the person, context, and time aspects of the model. The person component comprises genetic and individual characteristics such as personal attitudes and beliefs, past experiences, mental and physical health, and the father's stress levels. Furthermore, just as father involvement and its effects are shaped by personal characteristics, they are also shaped by context. Indeed, Marsiglio, Roy, and Fox (2005) argued that fathering is best understood through the physical setting and social context in which it takes place. For example, among nonresident fathers, paying child support may be the most crucial part of involvement. In contrast, among middle-class fathers in dual-income families, healthy involvement may take the form of more equal parenting duties (Koivunen, Rothaupt, & Wolfgram, 2009). Finally, FI and its effects also vary with time, both in terms of the child's (Dyer, Day, & Harper, 2013) and father's age (Y. Lee, Fagan, & Chen, 2012).

Robin, Dyer, and Mc Bride (2019) state that Identity theory is an application of symbolic interactionism. It holds that father involvement is highly influenced by a man's conception of, and the salience of, his fatherhood identity. When it is reflected back to them that they have met their standard, they feel "verified" in their identity. Because identity standards form part of a person's overall self-concept, individuals are motivated to act in ways that meet their identity standards (Stryker & Burke, 2000). Men with higher father role centrality at the birth of their child have higher relationship quality with their children (Adamsons, 2013). Also, men who view their nurturer role as important are more likely to be involved with their children (Rane & McBride, 2000). By focusing specifically on the lived experiences of fathers with huge responsibility when they are prominent figures who also have to spend their time for society, this study seeks to further our understanding of:

1. How was the upbringing process experienced?
2. How did they determine their parenting philosophy and practices regarding their role as prominent figures in society?"

It was necessary to know this experience to give information for fathers practicing their role in child-rearing.

3 Method

Researchers used a qualitative design to provide a detailed exploration of the lived experiences of prominent figures who hold important positions in society and also fathers of more than two children. In accordance with this aim, data were collected through in-depth semi-structured interviews and implementing interpretative phenomenological analysis (IPA). IPA was chosen to identify personal perceptions and subjective meanings of the disclosure process experienced by the intimate partners (Smith et al., 2009).

3.1 Samples

The participants in this study were two individuals who hold important positions in society. One of them is a leader in an academic position, and the other one is a leader in a youth community organization. Following the interpretative phenomenological approach, we used a small and purposively selected sample of participants who had the experience of the phenomenon being studied, which is their role as fathers (Smith et al., 2009). Furthermore, typical sample sizes for phenomenological studies range from 1 to 10 participants (Trinidad & Starks, 2007). The two participants conformed to four inclusion criteria: (a) fathers, (b) have more than two children, (c) hold important position in society, and (d) have little time with family.

3.2 Measurement Tool

Researchers developed an in-depth semi-structured interview using specific guidelines according to the research questions to learn about the participant's lived experiences as fathers. The interviewer probed about the interviewee's feelings, thoughts, and behaviors. Two investigators conducted face-to-face interviews; each interview was conducted individually for 120 to 210 minutes (in few times each). All interviews were audio-recorded and transcribed verbatim.

3.3 Data Analysis

Analyzing each transcript allowed the researchers to be open to new themes from each participant, rather than being driven by themes from previous transcripts. The initial codes were then translated into emergent themes, and connections were made between the themes. In the next stage, the themes for each participant were merged; this process underwent several rearrangements until the final themes were decided upon. To increase the trustworthiness and credibility of the analysis, the two researchers (authors) audited the analysis separately by reading through transcripts and comparing these to the initial analysis (Yardley, 2008). They ensured that the identified themes were evidenced in the transcripts (Smith et al., 2009).

4 Results

There were five emergent themes and two superordinate themes concluded in this research:

4.1 Establishing Fathering Philosophy

Compromising their parents' past parenting. Two participants felt their parents' parenting style was responsible but in rigid and less affectionate ways. They interpreted this as a unique way to show their love but not the way that they choose to father their children.

Participant 1 felt his father's love because his father fulfilled the children's needs, took care of them, and thought about their futures. However, he later learned that kind of way was not effective in building his own family. Participant 2 felt his father's love from the positive values he taught. But, he felt that his father did not have much time to bond with all 12 children. He later learned that his friends' families had different ways of parenting. From all those experiences, he began to build a few ways of fathering that he would implement when he had children.

> "I have seen how my friend's family communicated and built such a warm relationship. Maybe it was because her family was not as extended as mine, and they were able to comfort each other. I also observed how my older siblings educated their children. Their ways were slightly different from how our father treated us. As I grew up, I was able to interpret my future parenting pattern."
> "My father was not too affectionate. He was not a talkative person as well. So we did not engage in deep conversation. But when he took care of his sick wife or children, I knew he loved his family. But I realize that I need to be affectionate to my children and I also have to be able to communicate with them in an intimate way."

Religious point of view. The two participants built their philosophy of fathering based on religious values. The religious values are based on Islamic values: (a) decency comes first, (b) having sciences and knowledge followed by practicing it in decent ways, (c) practicing religious rituals (praying and reading the Holy Quran), (d) duplicate how the prophet Muhammad SAW parenting, which is not to scream, not to hurt, and always communicate in tender ways, (e) and setting a man's figure in children's life.

> "My Father taught me that decency comes first and then having sciences and knowledge followed by practicing it in decent ways, practicing religious rituals (praying and reading the Holy Quran). I learned how the prophet Muhammad SAW parenting, which is not to scream, not to hurt, and always communicate in tender ways with our children."

4.1 Implementing the Fathering Ways

I am able. Both of the participants have the efficacy of implementing their parenting plan. Both of them have enormous energies and are supported by their personality traits. Participant 1 perceived himself as an affectionate and sensitive figure who loves children and easily forgets bad experiences. Participant 2 perceived himself as a nurturing and responsible individual. Many of his life experiences shaped him to be a strong person who can see the silver lining from his bad experiences. These qualities make them able to conquer obstacles in their ways.

Both of the participants assessed their children's abilities, problems, and personalities. They gave many efforts in supporting their children in achieving their potentials and also monitored their children's behaviors.

> "Since I basically like children, I love them. I really think I have what it's called... talent... talent to tenderly approach the children, to explore them, to make them comfortable. I can say that I am sensitive and caring. On the other side, I thank God that I easily forget the bad memories so that I didn't feel bad emotion or revengeful feeling towards bad experience."
> "We discuss interests, hobbies, and everything they want to talk about with them (children)."

Making the impossible, possible. Both of the participants were making time in most of the impossible time. They were making strategies to meet and bond with their children in such enormous activities.

> "I had a commitment with myself, even if I felt exhausted, if the children wanted to play with me, I would not complain and I would play with them until I tucked them to bed."
> "I took my children to my office if I had to work on the weekend, so at least we were able to pray together on praying time, able to eat together on mealtime, and I got to see their faces."

Wife supports. They admitted that their wives have important roles in implementing their fathering values to the children. Participant 1 perceived his wife as his "emotional guardian." His wife provided him with emotional equilibrium. This equilibrium state makes him a better person and father. Participant 2 perceived his wife as an obedient wife who can accept and respect him with his parenting values.

> "My wife is my emotion regulator. So when I have a negative emotion, she could turn my emotion down, so I got to be able to face my children with positive emotion."
> "My wife is an obedient wife, so she could commit with the agreement on how we are going to educate our children together, so this is a big help for me to form my fathering way to our children."

5 Conclusion

In conclusion, these prominent father figures can manage their responsibilities as fathers in spite of their enormous activities in their communities because of these qualities: first, they were processing a phase where they decided on how they wanted to raise their children based on their upbringing experiences. They have a very clear standard on building the rules of fathering based on Islamic religious values. This finding validated that cultures determine people's views of fathering (Gonzalez-Mena, 2008; Izumi-Taylor, Lee, & Franceschini, 2011) and influence their values, beliefs, and attitudes (Fagan & Palm, 2004; Ito & Izumi-Taylor, 2013). Second, they have the efficacy, the energies, and the abilities to perform their fathering plan. This result was supported by the finding that states men with higher father role centrality at the birth of their child have higher relationship quality with their children (Adamsons, 2013). Third, they were also making strategies to make time for their children. It has been proven that young fathers' involvement in child-rearing has increased. Fathers spend more time with their children and show an increased interest in quality interactions (Jo & Park 2017). Fourth, they perceived that their wives' agreement on how they will rear the children as support. It proves that children's problems are no longer the mother's sole responsibility; instead, they are a common issue for both parents to attend to and deal with together (Hwang & Hwang, 2014). They also perceived that their role in child-rearing was significant. The new concept of fathers shown in this result was being strengthened by the conclusion offered by Robin, Dyer, and Mc Bride (2019) that father roles were a new emphasis on equal parenting.

6 Affiliations

1. Name: Indri Utami Sumaryanti
Institution: Faculty of Psychology, Universitas Islam Bandung
Address: Jl. Taman Sari No. 1 Bandung, West Java, Indonesia
E-mail: indri.utami@unisba.ac.id

2. Name: Fanni Putri Diantina
Institution: Faculty of Psychology, Universitas Islam Bandung
Address: Jl. Taman Sari No. 1 Bandung, West Java, Indonesia
E-mail: fanni.putridiantina@unisba.ac.id

7 References

Adamsons, K. (2013). A longitudinal investigation of mother's and father's initial fathering identities and later father-child relationship quality. *Fathering: A Journal of Theory, Research, and Practice About Men as Fathers, 11,* 118–137. http://dx.doi.org/10/3149/fth.1102.118

Baldwin, J., Faulkner, S., Hecht, M., & Lindsley, S. (2006). *Redefining culture.* Mahwah, NJ: Erlbaum.

Cabinet Office of Japan. (2009). A 2009 declining birthrate white paper, chapter countermeasures against a declining birthrate. Retrieved from http://www8.cao.go.jp/shoushi/whitepaper/english/w-2009

Cabrera, N. J., Fitzgerald, H. E., Bradley, R. H., & Roggman, L. (2014). The ecology of father-child relationship: An expanded model. *Journal of Family Theory Review, 6,* 336–354.

Chen, Y. (2002, July 3). "Press" fathers stay with their kinds. *Wuhan Daily.* Retrieved from: http://www.cnhan.com/gb/content/2002-07/03/content_183840.htm

Dyer, W., Day, R. D., & Harper, J. M. (2013). Wrestling Proteus: Assessing the varying nature of father involvement across contexts. *Journal of Marriage and Family, 75,* 837–857. http://dx.doi.org//10.1111/jomf.12036

Fagan, J., & Palm, G. (2004). *Fathers and early childhood programs.* Clifton Park, NY: Thomson Delmar Learning.

Gonzalez-Mena, J. (2008). *Diversity in early care and education* (4th ed.). New York, NY: McGraw-Hill.

Hwang, S. S., & Hwang, H. S. (2014). The relationship between early childhood fathers' parenting efficacy and parenting involvement. *Journal of Cognitive Enhancement and Intervention, 5,* 71–93.

Ito, Y., & Izumi-Taylor, S. (2013). A comparative study of fathers' thoughts about fatherhood in the USA and Japan. *Early Child Development and Care, 183*(11), 1689–1704. doi:10.1080/03004430.2012.746969

Izumi-Taylor, S., Lee, Y., & Franceschini, L. (2011). A comparative study of child-care in Japan and the US: Who needs to take care of youngsters? *Early Child Development and Care, 181*(1–2), 39–54.

Jo, J. S., & Park, J. H. (2017). The effects of mothers' parenting stress on children's problematic behavior: the moderating effects of fathers' parenting participation. *Global Creative Leader, 7,* 1–20.

Kim, J. H., & Lee, S. N. (2014). The ideals and practices of fatherhood among highly educated and married males in their 30s. *Family and Culture, 26,* 71–104.

Koivunen, J. M., Rothaupt, J. W., & Wolfgram, S. M. (2009). Gender dynamics and role adjustment during the transition to parenthood: Current perspective. *The Family Journal, 17*(3), 23–328. http://dx/doi.org/10.1177/1066480709347360

Lamb, M. E. (1986). The changing roles of fathers. In M. E. Lamb (Ed.), *The father's role: Applied perspectives* (pp. 18–35). New York, NY: John Wiley.

LaRossa, R. (1997). *The modernization of fatherhood: A social and political history*. Chicago, IL: University of Chicago Press.

Lee, Y., Fagan, J., & Chen, W.-Y. (2012). Do late adolescent fathers have more depressive symptoms than older fathers? *Journal of Youth and Adolescence, 41,* 1366–1381. http://dx.doi.org/10.1007/s10964-011-9717-8

Marsiglio, W., Roy, K., & Fox, G. L. (2005). *Situated fathering.* Lanham, MD: Rowman & Littlefield.

Ministry of Health, Labour and Welfare of Japan. (2011). Promotion to support the balance between work and family life. Retrieved from http://www.mhlw.go.jp/english/policy/children/workfamily/dl/psbbwfl.pdf

Rane, T. R., & McBride, B. A. (2000). Identity theory as a guide to understanding father's involvement with their children. *Journal of Family Issues, 21*, 347–366. htpp://dx.doi.org/10.1177/019251300021003004

Robin, N., Dyer, & Mcbride. (2019). *Fathers: Contemporary family psychology: Vol. I Foundation, methods and contemporary issues across the life span.* APA (Chapter 30). Http://dx.doi.org/10.1037/0000099-030

Stryker, S., & Burke, P. J. (2000). The past, present, and future of an identity theory. *Social Psychology Quarterly, 63,* 284–297. http://dx.doi.org/10.2307/2695840

Islamic Psychology and Biopsychological Basics of Life in Education and Health

Edited by Dian Sari Utami, Emi Zulaifah and Marcus Stueck

Volume 1 Wanadya Ayu Krisna Dewi / Emi Zulaifah / Dian Sari Utami / Marcus Stueck (eds.): Islamic Psychology - Integrative Dialogue. Psychology, Spirituality, Science and Arts. 2023.

Volume 2 Muhammad Ali Ramdhani / Agus Abdul Rahman / Nani Nuranisah Djamal / Asti Meiza (eds.): Family in Islamic Psychology Perspective: Challenges and Solutions. 2023.

www.peterlang.com

www.ingramcontent.com/pod-product-compliance
Ingram Content Group UK Ltd.
Pitfield, Milton Keynes, MK11 3LW, UK
UKHW020152290926
15471UKWH00005B/834